Christian Pharisees

*The Striking Similarities
of America's Conservative Christians
and Jesus' Earthly Enemies*

James Butcher

A free small group Bible study
based on
Christian Pharisees
is available on
www.ChristianPharisees.com

To Karen, of course

www.ChristianPharisees.com

Copyright 2017 by James Butcher

All rights reserved. No portions of this book may be reproduced in any manner without the written permission of the author except in the case of brief quotations embodied in articles and reviews.

Table of Contents

Introduction
1

Chapter One
"Why Does Your Teacher Eat With Sinners?"
Compassion, tax collectors, and holiness by separation
9

Chapter Two
"Whoever Exalts Himself Shall Be Humbled"
Pride, public faith, and phylacteries
25

Chapter Three
"[They] Will Take Away Both Our Place and Our Nation"
Power, politics, and the culture war
47

Chapter Four
"A People Who Will Produce Its Fruit"
Empty belief, a dead tree, and a productive life
67

Chapter Five
"He Who Is Forgiven Little Loves Little"
Respectability, "good people," and Plan B
97

Chapter Six
"You Are Israel's Teacher
and Do You Not Understand These Things?"
Nicodemus, the basics, and Paul's theological masterpiece
111

Chapter Seven
"You Do Not Know the Scriptures"
Bible study, misplaced confidence, and Tiny Tim
131

Chapter Eight
"The Tradition of the Elders"
*Your Sunday best, C.E.O. pastors,
and a "personal relationship with Jesus"*
147

Chapter Nine
"Lovers of Money"
Consumerism, greed, and America's greatest sin
167

Chapter Ten
"Woe to You, You Hypocrites"
Scorched earth, dirty dishes, and whitewashed tombs
187

Epilogue
"[They] Rejected God's Purpose for Themselves"
Repentance, John the Baptist, and what's next
209

Endnotes
217

Introduction

There are stories you hear that quickly pass from your mind. There are others, though, that linger with you, that speak to a deeper truth, that echo a hope or hurt in your own heart. These are the stories to which you return again and again. One such story for me is told by the great evangelical author Philip Yancey.

A friend of Philip's was working with the poor and broken in Chicago. A prostitute came to him seeking help in buying food for her two-year-old daughter. She confessed to Philip's friend not only the prostitution, but other dark sins in her life. After talking for a while, he tried to point her toward Christ:

> At last I asked if she had ever thought of going to a church for help. I will never forget the look of pure, naïve shock that crossed her face. "Church!" she cried. "Why would I ever go there? I was already feeling terrible about myself. They'd just make me feel worse."[1]

When you read the gospels, it is telling how often Jesus is surrounded by the outcasts, the disenfranchised, the shunned, the struggling, the *sinners*. There are a number of reasons for this, but the compassion they felt from Him is certainly near the top of the list. Conservative Christians claim to be passionate representatives of Jesus in American culture, yet the Yancey story speaks powerfully that churches are not the first place to which sinners turn, but often among the last.

When I talk to my Christian friends, I sometimes say something like, "The church today is just not what it is supposed to be." I *always* get an agreeing response. Usually the person will nod his head and quietly say, "I know" or "You're right." There is widespread acknowledgement among Christians that *something* is not right, though no agreement as to what the specific problem is.

This book is an attempt to provide a specific diagnosis of what is wrong with the church in America. At its core, my argument is fairly simple: during Jesus' ministry His main earthly enemy was the Pharisees; the Bible tells us quite a bit about the characteristics and priorities of the Pharisees; if Christians share the same traits as the Pharisees, it is indisputable proof that Christians have gotten wildly off track from God's will. I intend to prove that modern American Christians look frighteningly like the Pharisees. Is the church in America full of *Christian disciples* or *Christian Pharisees*?

My History as a Conservative Christian

The focus of this book is on the conservative Protestant segment of the church in America. It is a group with which I have identified my entire adult life. It will be helpful for you to know my background as you read this book.

I was saved on a youth trip to a gospel presentation and baptized in an American Baptist church as a teenager. I soon became involved in various ministries in that home church. My career goal was to become a lawyer, but I felt called to be a pastor. I fought that for a while, but eventually pursued God's call. I attended a Southern Baptist seminary – partly because it was a good school and partly because it was reasonably close to where my fiancée lived. After three years there, I began pastoring. I have pastored three churches over the last twenty years – two traditional churches and a church plant.[2] Throughout all this, being a conservative Christian has been a strong part of my identity.

In sum, I have been a conservative Christian for more than thirty years and a conservative Christian pastor for more than twenty. In many ways it has been a wonderful experience. This book is not an angry diatribe against a group of people I hate. I have so many friends who are conservative Christians and much of my life is bound up in conservative Christian ideas.

How much has my life been defined by conservative Christianity? I know why it is important to go to the altar. I know what the Roman Road is. I know that everyone thinks Charles Stanley is great. I know the differences between NIV, ESV, NASB, NLT, and NKJV. I know what a Thompson chain-reference is. I know the importance of having John MacArthur commentaries, even if you do not agree with all his theology. I know the difference between "Imagine" and "I Can Only Imagine." I know how little prayer happens at Wednesday Night Prayer Meeting. I know what true love does. I know *Lead Me On* was more culturally significant, but *A Liturgy, a Legacy & a Ragamuffin Band* is the best CCM album of all time. I know what CCM means. I listened to Dr. James Dobson and co-host Mike Trout on "Focus on the Family." I read Chuck Colson books in order to have a Biblical worldview. I know what dispensationalism is. I know that Billy Graham, though once controversial, is now untouchable. I have called conservative Christianity home for thirty years.

This book is not meant to impugn the intentions of my conservative Christian friends. I believe most are sincerely pursuing what they believe to be God's path. They have simply been misinformed. Like countless other times over the last two thousand years, the church again needs a push back in the right direction after taking its eyes off God.

The Purpose of This Book

This book makes some stark accusations against conservative Christians. The truth needs to be spoken, even though it will hurt. My goal, though, is not punitive, but redemptive. My desire is that Christians would acknowledge the truth of these arguments and change their beliefs and behavior.

This book is primarily descriptive rather than prescriptive. In the last chapter, I will share one point that I think is important going forward, but that represents a minority of the book. The majority of the writing examines the ways that conservative Christians look like the Pharisees. I will unpack those from the Biblical record and then consider whether the revealed problem is also true of conservative Christians. In each case, the answer is yes.

Within these arguments, I am taking the approach to the Bible that conservative Christians do: that it is a reliable account of what happened in Jesus' day. Certainly there are scholars who question the accuracy of the Biblical account and the portrayal of the Pharisees and others therein. To cite just one:

> In all cases the gospel authors have woven Jesus' opponents into a dramatic narrative which is controlled by their purposes in writing the narrative rather than by a desire to faithfully reproduce the events of Jesus' life. Thus the Pharisees, scribes and Sadducees undergo mutation for dramatic and theological purposes.[3]

This book does not share that view. Rather, it treats the Bible as the reliable, trustworthy Word of God. Throughout this book, therefore, I will quote the Bible presuming what it shares is accurate and will refer to Jesus, God the Father, and the Holy Spirit with capitalized pronouns.

This book falls into the tradition of the Old Testament prophet. There are two primary ideas that come to mind concerning a prophet. The first is someone who predicts the future. I will not be doing that. The second is the prophet as a spokesman entrusted with an unwelcome message from God. In the Old Testament, Israel often strayed from God's will, so God repeatedly sent messages of rebuke (and ultimately hope) through His prophets. Sometimes the message was not well received and the prophet ended up ignored, thrown into a well, or even killed. At other times, though, the people recognized their error, heeded the divine message, and repented. I see this book along those lines. I believe that Christians have strayed from God's desire and are in need of rebuke and a change in direction. My sincere prayer is that the hard truths within this book find tender hearts, acknowledgement of substantial mistakes, and an openness to move along better paths. I am acutely aware, though, that these truths may instead bring responses of anger, accusation, and dismissal. Ultimately, the prophet's job is to share the message; the response is up to the people. I hope I have faithfully delivered the message I believe God desires to be shared. If I have, may the Holy Spirit speak with conviction through this book; if I have not, may nothing come of it.

A Few Definitions

The main audience for this book are people identifying by a number of different labels: "evangelical," "conservative Christian," "Bible-believing Christian," "born-again Christian," and "fundamentalist." Throughout most of my adult life I have personally identified most closely with the term "evangelical." The definition that George Barna uses for "evangelicals" is one that defines all the above labels fairly well:

> Have made a personal commitment to Jesus Christ that is still important in their life today and believe that, when they die, they will go to heaven because they have confessed their sins and accepted Jesus Christ as their savior.... [Additional identifiers are] saying their faith is very important in their life today; believing they have a personal responsibility to share their religious beliefs about Christ with non-Christians; believing that Satan exists; believing that Jesus Christ lived a sinless life on earth; asserting that the Bible is accurate in all that it teaches; believing that eternal salvation is possible only through grace, not works; and describing God as the all-knowing, all-powerful, perfect deity who created the universe and still rules it today.[4]

For the most part throughout this book, I will simply use the term "Christian." Of course, I know that "Christian" includes Protestant, Catholic, and Orthodox; within Protestantism, it encompasses both mainline and more conservative denominations. As I am using the term "Christian" in this book, I am focusing on the conservative Protestant elements of the faith, although others are certainly welcome to see where my arguments apply to their lives.

American conservative Christians have been quick to point out the shortcomings of other parts of the Christian world (as well as the unsaved world around us) but have largely been blind to our own failures. *Christian Pharisees* argues that we are out of God's will in serious and profound ways. This book is not an attempt to point a finger at others and say they have gotten it wrong – it is an admission of error on my own part as well as those who are like me. This book is an act of penance. As the pastor of my youth often said, "I'm drawing the circle and standing inside it."

With that in mind, I want to admit up front that I am not perfectly living out all the ideas in this book. It took a long time to get where we are; it will take a long time to get someplace better. I also want to acknowledge that with every point, I understand that there are inevitably exceptions to what I am saying. Somewhere there are Christians who are getting it right. It would be too tedious to refer to "Christians in general" throughout the book.

Finally, a brief word on a few terms that will recur throughout the book. Specifically, the differences between parties and roles. The Pharisees were one of the several religious parties of Jesus' day. Other ones included the Sadducees and Herodians. A rough equivalent to our day would be denominations. We will talk throughout the book about the specifics that the Pharisees believed (and a little about the other parties), but the important thing for now is that each person could only be a member of one party. Just as someone who is a Baptist is by definition not a Pentecostal, so too someone who was a Pharisee was by definition not a Sadducee or Herodian. Those groups each held different sets of beliefs. I will also refer to several roles, like scribe, chief priest, and lawyer. Those are jobs or positions that people had in Jesus' day. You could be a scribe and be a Pharisee; you could be a scribe and be a Sadducee. Pharisee or Sadducee was your *party* but scribe was your *role*.

Acknowledgements

I am thankful to have friends and colleagues who submitted themselves to the strenuous task of reading drafts of this book and offering insightful critique: Mason Ballard, Melissa Ballard, Shelly Brooks, Don Davis, Paula Davis, Beth Hager, Max Hill, Lawrence

Hoptry, Bob Humphrey, David King, Brenda Lathey, Rod Lathey, Jason Lutz, Lois Merritt, Ellin Ramsey, Bill Robinson, John Simmons, Brian Stewart, Kathy Stewart, Ron Stoner, Chris Swindell, Chad Watson, Elizabeth Withers, and Michael Young. Their assistance was invaluable. I am also indebted to the pastors of the Colloquium, who provided helpful critique and encouragement.

I am thankful to Tatlin for the cover design. Their provocative image conveys how small a change it takes for something that is supposed to represent Christ (like the crown of thorns; like Christians) to become something darker.

I am thankful for the help I received from Ellin Ramsey in formatting portions of the book.

I am thankful for Tom Thomas' assistance in creating the website associated with this book. I am thankful for Christie Barnhart's photographic work in those efforts.

I am thankful for the encouragement that I have received from my church.

Finally, I have been blessed by the steadfast support of my wife in this endeavor. I love her more than words can convey. It is to her that I dedicate this book.

Chapter One

"Why Does Your Teacher Eat With Sinners?"

Compassion, tax collectors, and holiness by separation

Years ago, for my wife's thirtieth birthday, several of her friends wrote her letters on what she had meant to them. One of the most powerful was written by a male friend who came out as homosexual when they were in college. Their group of friends mostly consisted of Christians and this news led to many severed and destroyed relationships. Here is what he wrote to Karen a decade after the fact:

> School, family, church, friends – everything was shaken to the core. Nothing would ever be the same again and some things would be gone for good! Except one thing – a funny, compassionate, warm-hearted friend. You didn't leave my life! Your friendship was the first experience with unconditional love that I had ever had in my life. You seemed to offer this friendship with such a natural grace and ease. Your compassionate disposition took over, offering me not "Christian" love but a genuine, selfless "Christlike" love.

His words (used with his permission) are painful for me to read because I have to acknowledge that for substantial portions of my younger life my response would have been less like Karen's and more like her friends. I hope over the years I have become more like her and therefore more like Jesus.

This chapter focuses on a lengthy passage in Matthew 9 that cuts to the heart of the difference between Jesus and Christians on this point. This larger passage is composed of several pieces, with the first story being the most important. The focus is on Jesus' response to "sinners." By "sinners" here, I am using the common usage within Christian circles, where the term is a catchall for people who are away from God. Of course, Christians will note as a follow-up that everyone is a sinner as long as we are in this fallen world, but its use to refer to the spiritually lost is nonetheless frequent. One of the more glaring differences between Christians and Jesus is that sinners liked being with Jesus. Christians? Not so much.

"The Sinners . . . Were Dining with Jesus"

Our story opens in Matthew 9:9:

> As Jesus went on from there, He saw a man called Matthew, sitting in the tax collector's booth; and He said to him, "Follow Me!" And he got up and followed Him.[1]

Matthew was an Israelite and a tax collector. That made him a despised man. True Israelites like the Pharisees saw him as a sellout working for the oppressive Roman government. Further, rarely were tax collectors honest in their work, often extorting a little extra for themselves as they did their job. To the Pharisees' thinking, this would make Matthew a terrible choice of someone with whom to associate, let alone to call to be one of your main disciples. Jesus, however, did exactly that, not only calling Matthew to be His disciple ("Follow Me!"), but actually calling him while he was collecting taxes. Perhaps equally surprising to the Pharisees' way of thinking, Matthew accepted the call and obeyed Christ.

The following verse tells us that Matthew had a meal at his house ("While Jesus was having dinner at Matthew's house . . ."[2]) and invited his friends to come meet Jesus:

> many tax collectors and sinners came and were dining with Jesus and His disciples.[3]

This strikes me as a particularly beautiful scene. All of these people who had long felt distant from God because they were functioning under the Pharisees' rules of engagement find themselves welcomed and wanted by this prophet from Nazareth. Equally important, impressive, and beautiful, all indications are that Jesus wanted to be with them. They were the tax collectors – the despised, compromised betrayers of their fellow Israelites, but for some reason this Jesus fellow was willing to sit with them, eat with them, talk with them, laugh with them, listen to them. They were the "sinners" – used the same way Christians use it today – caught up in various spiritual struggles, unwanted at the Temple, shunned at synagogue, but for some reason Jesus did not reject them the way the Pharisees and religious leaders commonly did. I wonder how their hearts felt to sit at a meal with this Man who was clearly God's representative and yet liked and welcomed them?

Jesus' behavior toward these people made absolutely no sense, though, to the Pharisees. Incredulous, they approached and asked His disciples:

> "Why is your Teacher eating with the tax collectors and sinners?"[4]

You can hear the consternation in their voices. It is not even that they came initially to accuse; it is more that they simply could not comprehend why He would do this. They have no category for this. It did not fit in any of their theological boxes. It just made *no sense* to them.

Why was it so difficult for them to comprehend? The primary reason is that the Pharisees practiced what I call *holiness by separation*. How important was separation to the Pharisees? The name

"Pharisees" actually means "separated ones," so this was central to their belief and identity.[5]

The Pharisees were not God-haters. In fact, they were passionate in their devotion to following Him. The problem was they put the wrong things at the center of their faith. Their interpretation of the Old Testament Law caused them to believe two things relevant to this point. First, to honor God they needed to be personally holy. Second, to achieve that holiness, they needed to keep themselves separate from the sinful things of this world. For the Pharisees, this came to include staying away from the impure, the downtrodden, the unclean, and the unholy. It simply made no sense to them why a teacher who claimed to represent God and to be holy would allow Himself to be surrounded by so many sinful people.

We find a similar sentiment expressed by Simon the Pharisee in Luke 7. In that situation, a woman "who was a sinner" came to Jesus while He ate at Simon's house.[6] The woman proceeded to anoint Jesus' feet with expensive perfume.[7] The Pharisee could not comprehend why Jesus allowed this:

> Now when the Pharisee who had invited Him saw this, he said to himself, "If this man were a prophet He would know who and what sort of person this woman is who is touching Him, that she is a sinner."[8]

Again, Jesus allowing the sinful person near Him made no sense to the Pharisee's way of thinking.

Back at Matthew the tax collector's meal, Jesus overheard the Pharisees' question and decided to take it Himself. His words form this chapter's central point:

> "It is not those who are healthy who need a physician, but those who are sick. But go and learn what this means: 'I desire compassion, and not sacrifice,' for I did not come to call the righteous, but sinners."[9]

Wow – there is a revolution right there in those few words.

The beginning and ending statements point out for whom Jesus came to this earth. He came on a rescue mission. He came for the "sick." He came for the "sinners." This, of course, ties perfectly into the verse (John 3:17) that is right after the most famous verse in the Bible:

> "For God did not send the Son into the world to judge the world, but that the world might be saved through Him."[10]

Jesus' purpose was not to condemn, but to offer hope. His purpose was not tell people how bad they were, but that redemption was possible. His purpose was not to proclaim how eager God was for judgment, but for repentance.

More important, though, is the heart of that statement:

> "'I desire compassion, and not sacrifice.'"[11]

What is the thing for which the heart of God longs? Compassion. In this context, it clearly means compassion toward those who are broken, sinful, messy, and lost. The heart of God delights in compassion toward them. Most scholars believe that the second half of the statement is best understood as "more than sacrifice." It is not that Jesus is saying that His followers will never have to sacrifice for Him. In fact, several hearing these words at this dinner will literally die for Him. Rather, Jesus is saying that compassion needs to be at the center.

The problem with the *holiness by separation* idea is not that holiness or separation are irrelevant ideas. There is a place within spiritual lives for holiness – God does want His people to be less sinful and to be more like Him. There is a place within spiritual lives for separation – there may be times a believer has to remove himself from a situation for one reason or another. The problem was that the Pharisees had put *holiness by separation* at the center of their faith in how they dealt with the people around them. When they encountered those who seemed to be distant from God, the center of their response was *holiness by separation*.

Here Jesus tells us what He wants at the center of His followers' faith when it comes to those who are distant from God: *compassion*. That is the guiding principle. When you see the woman mired in sexual sin, Jesus wants your first response to be compassion. When you encounter the homeless man who is clearly half-wasted, Jesus wants your first response to be compassion. When you talk to that co-worker who loves to spout atheist rhetoric half because he believes it and half to get a rise out of you, Jesus wants your first response to be compassion. When you see on the news the woman walking out of the abortion clinic, Jesus wants your first response to be compassion.

Does the person deserve it? Perhaps not, but Jesus' earthly mission never was, thank God, about our getting what we deserve. It was about *compassion*.

This approach is not indicative of Christians' response to sinners. (Understatement of the year?) Christians are sorely lacking in compassion.

Christians are more known by who and what they are against than whom and what they support. Christians lead with judgment and presume that mercy and grace must follow much later. Christians consistently fail to have the right thing at the center in their dealings with sinners. Remember the Philip Yancey story with which I began the book? "I was already feeling terrible about myself. They'd just make me feel worse." This is the reputation of followers of Jesus?

Why did the tax collectors and sinners *want* to eat with Jesus? It is really not that complicated. It was *the compassion that Jesus had for them*. He genuinely loved them. He delighted in sharing mercy. He was quick with a word of grace. He did not look at them as people who could be loved by God if they made major life changes; He saw them as people who were already desperately loved by God. *Of course they wanted to eat with Him*! Who wouldn't? Under such conditions, who among us would not delight in every moment with Him?

Christians have failed spectacularly in this regard. They have somehow managed to become the people that sinners least want to be near. They have somehow managed to lose almost all sight of compassion and have inserted judgment and condemnation in its place.

A small thought experiment: what if Christians forgot all their larger culture war concerns, all their passion for "winning America back," all their good reasons for condemning "those people" and for the next decade made compassion their central thought toward those who are away from God? What if they did not obsessively debate whether doing so might be perceived as accommodating sin or might not be sufficiently conservative? What if they just led with compassion in every encounter with people who are away from God?

Fasting and New Wineskins

The compassion theme continues throughout the remainder of Matthew 9. Immediately after the "I desire compassion" interaction, though, there are a couple statements by Jesus that do not immediately seem connected. I believe they are and will explain why.

First, Jesus was asked by the disciples of John the Baptist why His followers did not fast regularly. He replied:

> "How can the guests of the bridegroom mourn while [He] is with them? The time will come when the bridegroom will be taken from them; then they will fast."[12]

The "bridegroom" here was Jesus. The church would be considered, in this analogy, his spiritual "bride."

The point for our purposes is straightforward: Jesus was saying this was an unusual time for His followers because He (the bridegroom) was still on earth. Once He was gone (i.e., ascended back into heaven forty days after His resurrection), He did expect His followers to do the things that normally make up a solid spiritual life, like fasting.

How is this relevant to the "I desire compassion" that came just before it? It would be the presumption of many who hear the Jesus' "compassion, not sacrifice" message that His intent included a lowering of moral standards and expectations for His followers. You can almost hear the Pharisees' thinking in response to Jesus' "I desire compassion" statement: "Sure You do – and we all know where this is leading: anything goes, just wink at sin, it's not their fault, just have a bleeding heart. Compassion really means compromised standards. Compassion really means excused sin. Compassion really means lower morality."

Matthew immediately turned to this fasting question to make it clear that compassion was not to be defined as "do whatever and God does not care." Jesus' heart was compassion as He saw those who were spiritually "sick" - He loved them even though they were in that state, but His love also meant that He wanted to see them made well. The gospel He preached was transformative. Matthew wanted to make it clear that compassion was not a code word for license to sin.

Second, Jesus continued with an interesting analogy:

> "No one sews a patch of unshrunk cloth on an old garment, for the patch will pull away from the garment, making the tear worse. Neither do people pour new wine into old wineskins. If they do, the skins will burst; the wine will run out and the wineskins will be ruined. No, they pour new wine into new wineskins, and both are preserved."[13]

This saying has been much-debated through the centuries, but in the context of this conversation, the meaning seems fairly straightforward. When we consider this "I desire compassion" teaching of Christ and the response He received from the least and the lost, it is an understatement to say that Jesus was ushering in a new era. That is true not only because of the new spiritual life that His death and resurrection would soon make possible, but also because of the message of mercy that He embodied. This was not a mild revision to the Old Testament system. Jesus was inaugurating a new era.

This too is important to understand in the context of the "I desire compassion" story. The Pharisees needed to know that this was not going to be business as usual. Jesus wanted a new paradigm –

something that reflected the heart of the Father. He wanted compassion to be the go-to emotion for His followers in dealing with those who were away from God.

In summary, the "I desire compassion" statement is immediately followed by two reminders. First, this compassion emphasis is not to be construed as an excuse to condone an undisciplined spiritual life ("when the bridegroom will be taken from them; then they will fast"). Second, this compassion emphasis does represent a new era in God's movement in the world. The Kingdom that Jesus is bringing to fruition is not a slightly varied continuation of the old Temple system.

Three Compassion Examples

The chapter continues on a compassion theme with three stories where Jesus showed compassion to hurting people, the chapter then closing with a final, important overarching compassion statement. In this section, we will briefly examine the three stories.

The first story is found in Matthew 9:18-26. It is actually a tale of two women who were in many ways polar opposites. A synagogue leader approached Jesus and begged Him to come and resurrect his daughter who had just died.[14] As Jesus and His disciples traveled with the man, a woman who had been physically suffering for more than a decade approached Jesus from behind, believing that if she touched His garment she would be healed.[15] Jesus noticed her, was impressed by her faith, and healed her.[16] He continued His journey to the synagogue leader's home, where He resurrected the young girl.[17]

The two women were a study in contrasts. One had been ceremonially unclean for years; the other by all indications had a healthy childhood. One was at the bottom of the social ladder; the other was the daughter of a community leader. Yet what they both shared was more important: a need for healing. In both cases, the healing came because of the compassion of Jesus.

In the second story, Jesus encountered two blind men. They were persistent in spite of their disability, as the Bible says they "followed Him, crying out, 'Have mercy on us, Son of David!'"[18] Expressing their belief that He had the power to heal them, Jesus "touched their eyes, saying, 'It shall be done to you according to your faith.'"[19] They were healed, with Jesus warning them to keep the news quiet.[20]

In the third story Jesus healed a demon-possessed man.[21] The crowd was amazed, but the Pharisees contended that He was casting out demons "by the ruler of the demons."[22] Even in His compassionate acts, Jesus received opposition.

In all, we see a variety of expressions of Jesus showing compassion to hurting and needy people.

Why Jesus Did It

As previously stated, the chapter ends by bringing together the theme of compassion. It also shares an unexpected and needed reminder concerning one of the key implications of failing to understand the merciful nature of this Kingdom.

This final section of Matthew 9 begins with a broad summary:

> Jesus was going through all the cities and villages, teaching in their synagogues and proclaiming the gospel of the kingdom, and healing every kind of disease and every kind of sickness.[23]

Here we essentially have Jesus' day-to-day to-do list. He traveled throughout Israel. He taught them the truths of the Kingdom and the hope of the gospel. He healed.

That tells us the *what* of His activities; what about the *why*? The next verse answers that for us:

> Seeing the people, He *felt compassion* for them, because they were distressed and dispirited like sheep without a shepherd.[24]

Here is the key reference to compassion that ties the end of this chapter to the earlier material. Jesus *"felt compassion"* for the crowds and that motivated His actions. This was true both for the teaching and for the healing. They needed instruction in how to live as well as having their immediate physical issues addressed. When Jesus looked over the teeming throng, He was not annoyed by them or overwhelmed with a desire to see them judged for their sins. He was filled with compassion for them. This, of course, is to be expected. If earlier He had emphasized that God had said "I desire compassion," then the One claiming to be His perfect representative would embody that compassion in His daily interactions.

The chapter concludes with an unexpected addendum:

> Then [Jesus] said to His disciples, "The harvest is plentiful, but the workers are few. Therefore beseech the Lord of the harvest to send out workers into His harvest."[25]

This passage is frequently cited by pastors as an impetus for higher expectations in evangelism. "Our church needs to have great goals as we reach out because Jesus said the harvest is plentiful!" It is also often used to place a little guilt on those same congregations. "If we are not seeing that harvest, maybe it is because we do not have enough workers! Jesus warned the workers would be few - will you be one of those laborers?"

This is certainly an evangelism passage, but what is rarely noted is the larger context. It is the concluding statement in a passage on *compassion*. It began with the "I desire compassion" story, had two clarifications about the nature of this compassion, emphasized by back-to-back-to-back compassion examples, and then concluded with the statement of Jesus' heart for the people: "compassion . . . because they were . . . like sheep without a shepherd." That initial "I desire compassion" story saw those who were away from God longing to be near Jesus, enjoying His company at a dinner at Matthew's house. Could it be that the missing piece in Christians' poor showing in evangelism is their lack of compassion? Could it be that they have turned evangelism into a canned presentation to be given like a sales pitch with little thought for the need to actually love the person to whom they are speaking? Could it be that even today the harvest is plentiful with many hearts that would respond to an outpouring of compassion, but such a flood is nowhere to be seen in conservative Christian churches? Could it be that what the lost are looking for is a taste of compassion when what Christians have been offering is a straight diet of truth? Could it be that even in Jesus' day the number of people willing to be "workers" following that approach were "few" and two millennia have not expanded the percentage who are open to following Jesus' compassionate lead, even if that is the key to evangelistic impact?

Christians and "Sacrifice"

Having detailed the needed emphasis on compassion, I want to return to the key statement in this passage and discuss its second half. In it, we find the approach that both the Pharisees and modern Christians frequently utilize. Jesus told the Pharisees: "I desire compassion, and not sacrifice."[26] We have explored the importance of compassion, but said little about the shortcomings of "sacrifice." There are two technical issues to get out of the way up front. First, it should again be noted that scholars understand the statement here as "I desire compassion more than sacrifice" as opposed to "I desire compassion and never want you to sacrifice." There are other passages that make it clear that inevitably there will be times when sacrifice is necessary within the Christian life.[27] Second, in the Old Testament the word sacrifice usually meant the physical death of an animal within the Temple system. That approach was no longer operational after the death of Christ. Nonetheless, the idea of bringing a costly sacrifice to the Lord, whether it be service, financial, or otherwise, is not far from it. The core idea of bringing a gift of value to the Lord remains the same.

So what is wrong with sacrifice? It is not intrinsically bad, but a problem is created when we say that more sacrifice equals a better believer in God. Making sacrifice the ultimate goal or the main measure of true followers routes us onto a downhill path to negative consequences.

One major problem is that the mission gets twisted to the exact opposite of the original intent. It is a telling juxtaposition: the Pharisees' incredulousness that Jesus would actually eat with sinners and, a mere two verses later, Jesus stating that compassion was not a peripheral issue but a core part of His vision for His Kingdom. Jesus said His very mission was to be near those who were spiritually sick. That meant this was not a side note, but at the heart of who He was and why He came to earth. By obvious extension, it should be at the heart of what God wants from those who speak for Him. Jesus was not just revealing His own heart here, but the heart of God.

By comparison, the Pharisees were shocked and dumbfounded that Jesus would even be near tax collectors and sinners. It just did not make any sense to them. It is important to understand that those thoughts arose from their religious thinking. Their convictions in that direction came from the way they understood God. They came to that conclusion not despite their religion but exactly because of it.

This is worth pondering. *Their faith had been twisted into something that led them to despise the very people they should have loved: those away from God.* Their faith had been twisted into something that led them to shun the very ones they should have been seeking. This is not a slight departure from the right path; it is embracing the exact opposite of the intended purpose.

In their passionate pursuit of greater sacrifice, they then were left to wonder why God had not answered their prayer for their nation. They could not be the problem - they were *sacrificing* so much for God! The only answer, then, was "them." The sinners and the tax collectors, the unwashed and unrepentant were holding God back from giving His blessing. The problem was caused by "them." Rather than the sinners being the heart of the mission, they became the scapegoats. The end result: the very people who should have been central to drawing lost people to God wanted nothing to do with them.

Do Christians do this? With great passion. I will discuss this at length in the chapter on power, so I will merely note here the ever-increasing divide that the culture war has created over the last forty years. That divide exists in large part due to Christians treating their political enemies as the scapegoats for the problems that America faces. Christians have attempted to beat them into submission with their thick leather-bound Bibles. Christians have believed that pursuing political power is a higher priority than extending personal compassion. Christians seem largely unbothered that their reputation is now one that repels sinners rather than drawing them the way that Christ did.

A second problem is that measuring holiness by sacrifice makes religion into a competition. When faith is measured by the level of sacrifice, being a true believer means being better than everyone else is. Inevitably, that will lead to a sense of spiritual superiority.

It might show up in how much a person sacrificially gives. "Almost no one gives 10 percent any more, but I still do." It might show up in how much a person sacrificially does. "I'm at the church just about every day." It might show up in how sacrificially faithful a person is. "I never miss a service." It might show up in how much Bible a person has sacrificially learned. "He knows more Scripture than anyone else in the congregation." It might show up in how sacrificially long or frequently a person prays. "I'm a prayer warrior." It might show up in a person's heart for worship. "She knows the words to every single song in the hymnal by heart."

Is the focus of faith on competition or compassion? Focusing on competition causes the believer to lose sight of caring for those around him. It even causes the believer to see the spiritual progress of those around him as something he has to outdo rather than something in which to rejoice.

Here again Christians are guilty. The "pillars of the church" often see themselves as the ones who are sacrificing the most in order to keep the church going. They see their endless sacrifice as certain proof of their spiritual maturity.

Turn Their Stomach

A question worthy of consideration as we close: do people mired in sin break your heart? Jesus noted that such folks were spiritually sick. Of course, that means they are not spiritually healthy – things are not as they should be. For many Christians, their standard response to those stuck in sin is to be appalled and offended by those people's actions. It is a stunning lack of spiritual vision: they are shocked and mortified that *sinners are acting like sinners*. What do you expect them to act like? If Christians believe that the power of the gospel is the only hope for transforming lives, then does it not follow that one should anticipate sinners acting in those ways? (Not approve, but nonetheless expect.) Would that not necessarily mean that those who have not yet experienced that hope would inevitably be caught in their sin?

Too many Christians make it abundantly clear that sinners turn their stomach. Just to cite one example, I could speak at great length on the callous, hurtful, unsympathetic, and mean statements I have heard concerning homosexuals from Christians who are the "three-services-a-week" people at their churches. Words without an ounce of compassion. Sadly, those statements come from those Christians not in spite of the fact that they are Christians, but exactly because they are Christians. That is how far Christians have gotten from the compassionate heart of Jesus in this regard.

Christians are too often disgusted by people mired in their sin. They are horrified by what they say and do. They are not only uninterested in developing a relationship with them; they do not even want to be in the same room as them. Few Christians have a broken heart for those who are away from God, stuck in sin, and living in moral malaise.

Toward those needing God, do Christians believe their default emotion should be compassion or condemnation? On this subject, Christians' similarity to the Pharisees is substantial. Christians desperately need to "go and learn what this means: 'I desire compassion, and not sacrifice.'"

Chapter Two

"Whoever Exalts Himself Shall Be Humbled"

Pride, public faith, and phylacteries

While I was attending seminary, a national Southern Baptist official taught one of my summer term classes. (I will allow him to remain nameless.) Overall, it was a good class, but there was one moment that stood out.

Throughout the class, it was repeatedly clear that he was highly impressed with himself and his thoughts. During one of his lectures in the large hall, the discussion was diverted to a connected subject. This official shared his view on that topic and then added, "Actually, I just wrote an article on that for a new study Bible that's coming out. The article is really good, even if I do say so myself."

One of the students raised his hand and asked, "Did you also write the article on humility for the study Bible?" To his credit (and fortunately for that student's grade), the official took the barb from the student and laughter from the class in good humor and moved on with his lecture.

The Pharisees' Pride

John the Baptist saw the Pharisees walking toward him in the distance and shouted at them with a name that was guaranteed not to endear: "You brood of vipers!"[1] Many from across the countryside had come out to be baptized by this wild-eyed prophet, but the vast majority of the Pharisees refused to humbly submit to his declaration.[2] After all, they were the experts in the Law, not John.

They were the leaders to whom the people had looked for generations for religious instruction. They were God's faithful remnant. They did not need some guy wearing camel hair telling them what to do.³

Such pride in being leaders of the "chosen people of Israel" made them unwilling to humble themselves and undergo a baptism of repentance. John cut straight to their prideful hearts with his rebuke:

> "And do not think you can say to yourselves, 'We have *Abraham as our father.*' I tell you that *out of these stones God can raise up children for Abraham.* The ax is already at the root of the trees, and every tree that does not produce good fruit will be cut down and thrown into the fire."⁴

The Pharisees deeply felt the importance of their place. As Israelites, they were the descendants of the patriarch Abraham. They were the chosen people. They were the nation through whom the Messiah would come. Yet all of this did not instill in them an awestruck sense of humility at being the undeserved recipients of such honors; instead, they were filled with pride at the place and position they occupied both within Israel and within history. The Pharisees were a proud people.

Jesus addressed the pride of the Pharisees most poignantly in three passages that all contain the same idea as their climax. In Matthew 23, Luke 14, and Luke 18, Jesus spoke words of rebuke to the Pharisees about their pride, ending each time with almost the exact same words:

> "Whoever exalts himself shall be humbled; and whoever humbles himself shall be exalted."⁵

In this chapter, we will examine these three passages, each time considering the accusations of Jesus toward the Pharisees on this issue of pride (and its corollary: a lack of humility). Each time we will also explore whether Christians today make analogous mistakes. We will also examine the spiritual principle Jesus conveyed when He repeatedly told His disciples that the exalted would be humbled but the humble exalted.

"Everything They Do for Men to See"

Matthew 23 is Jesus' longest sustained diatribe against the Pharisees. One major early section of that chapter focuses on their lack of humility. He begins with the biting critique:

> "Everything they do is done for men to see."[6]

If I were to summarize this critique in two words, it would be *public faith*. The Pharisees focused their faith on the aspects that allowed for a public expression and the subsequent desired praise from those around them. Jesus gave three illustrations of the *public faith* of the Pharisees.

The first was the Pharisees "make their phylacteries wide and the tassels on their garments long."[7] Since these refer to Jewish traditions that are obscure to most, we will take a moment to unpack the ideas. Phylacteries were small square boxes that contained a few of the key Old Testament Scriptures. The idea arose from passages where God instructed Israel to have the Law on their hands and foreheads as a reminder:

> "This observance will be for you like a sign on your hand and a reminder on your forehead that the law of the Lord is to be on your lips."[8]

This was taken to be a symbolic idea that the Law was to be on their minds (in their thoughts) and in their hands (in their actions) all the time. Over time, though, some began to take it as a literal and physical command: they should wear the Law on their foreheads and on their hands. By Jesus' day, this led to the Pharisees wearing phylacteries. It is likely they saw this strict reading of the passage as a sign of the seriousness of their commitment.

Obviously, this was a very public expression of one's faith. One could not look at a Pharisee without seeing these outward expressions of his devotion to God. That, in itself, becomes potentially problematic. Are you wearing phylacteries because it actually reminds you of your commitment to obeying the Law or are you wearing them because it reminds others of your faith?

The Pharisees' motive and goal in their wearing of phylacteries is obvious in Jesus' criticism: that they made their phylacteries wide. In other words, they did not just obey what they considered to be their obligation – they made sure they did it in a way that was clearly visible to everyone. They chose not only the interpretation of the Scriptural passage that promoted a public expression of their faith, they then pursued that public expression in as prominent a manner as possible.

One presumes that rabbis of the day would have assured their synagogues that such behavior was not an expression of pride of self but rather pride in God. "I am not ashamed of my God! I am not afraid for anyone to know where I stand!" "Some may wonder why I choose to wear such large phylacteries. It is because I want those around me to know that I think God is supposed to be *prominent* in my mind and actions at all times." "Why do some of you act as if you're embarrassed by this expression of your faith? Do not just fulfill the obligation – be proud of your faith in God!" It is easy to justify religious actions that are actually intended to show off someone's own impressive religion and mask it under the idea that the person is just proud of his God.

Jesus then noted that they made their garments' tassels long. This idea also has an origin story that points to the Old Testament:

> "Throughout the generations to come you are to make tassels on the corners of your garments, with a blue cord on each tassel. You will have these tassels to look at and so you will remember all the commands of the Lord."[9]

Here the idea was a small reminder of the need to be faithful to the Scripture's teaching. The blue cord on the tassel on the corner of their garments would be a reminder throughout their day to regularly refocus on obeying the Lord.

The Pharisees, though, had made their tassels "long." Clearly the problem was not that they had vision issues and could not see down to their feet. Making the tassel (and with it the blue cord) long served not as a better reminder to the person wearing it, but as a statement to those around him. "My heart for God is bigger than yours." "My passion for the commands of God is greater than yours." What was supposed to be a gentle reminder to the person wearing it to live out the Lord's commands was made into a harsh statement to those seeing the person wearing it: you do not take your faith as seriously as I do.

These both played to the Pharisees' religious pride. They saw themselves as the remnant of God, as the chosen children of God, as the leaders of God's nation. These two items, originally intended to be reminders to the person to have an increasing private devotion, had been corrupted by the Pharisees into public expressions of their superior faith. One presumes from Jesus' words that the very fact that they wore such things was meant by them as evidence of their impressive devotion. Presumably they did not see it as an attempt to elevate themselves; they thought it was an expression of how they elevated God. That was just another sign of their lack of spiritual awareness. They had converted their faith into an ongoing attempt to show how great they were, not how great God was.

The tension is exemplified in two statements Jesus made in the Sermon on the Mount. Soon after the Beatitudes, Jesus proclaimed:

> "Neither do people light a lamp and put it under a bowl. Instead they put it on its stand, and it gives light to everyone in the house. In the same way, let your light shine before men, that they may see your good deeds and praise your Father in heaven."[10]

In the following chapter, though, Jesus said something that initially does not seem to dovetail with that first statement:

> "Be careful not to do your 'acts of righteousness' before men, to be seen by them. If you do, you will have no reward from your Father in heaven."[11]

He then proceeded to give some examples: do not blow a trumpet when you give your synagogue gift, but do it secretly; do not pray on the street corners, but go behind closed doors; do not make it obvious when you are fasting, but wash your face and keep the fast between you and God. Some have argued that these two passages are contradictory. To my mind, they are easily reconciled. The second passage echoes the sentiments from Matthew 23 that we have been examining: do not perform your religious acts for people to see. Focus on what is behind the scenes, since that is where the heart of faith necessarily resides. As you do those behind the scenes things, you will begin to become a person of faith and hope. Your life will naturally exude a light that is not a public relations effort, but, like the moon, simply a reflection of a greater light. To put it simply if your private faith is where it needs to be, the public impact of your faith will happen naturally.

Are American Christians guilty of focusing on a *public faith*? Allow me to attempt to paraphrase Jesus' words here for this generation:

> They make their Bibles thick and their fish bumper stickers shiny.
>
> They make morning devotions look good on Instagram and fill their Facebook News Feed with verses written on pretty pictures.
>
> They make their church steeples the highest point in town and every small outreach worthy of praise in the bulletin.

Christians are proudly public about their faith. They will tell you it is part of "being a witness" and "shining your light." Certainly there is an extent to which any genuine faith is going to express itself publicly. The central issue here, though, is that the Pharisees were doing their religion in a way where "everything they do is done for men to see." The issue is not having a hidden faith, but who your audience is. The Pharisees' audience was those around them. A strong case can be made that is also Christians' audience.

Being able to go into Christians' minds and hearts and accurately evaluate their motives would be the best way to prove this, but that, of course, is impossible. A secondary way that we can evaluate the claim is with this question: how much is left of most Christians' faith when all that is visible is gone? Take away church on Sunday morning, where he might be going to be seen rather than because he truly wants to worship God. Take away that big leather-bound Bible that is laid out on her lap as the pastor preaches. Take away the Instagram pics and Facebook posts. What is left? How much actual time does he spend every day in private prayer with God? How often does she read that thick Bible when no one else is around? How many people does he financially help with no one knowing? What ways does she serve where no one can see? A strong argument can be put forth that Christians have made the things that define a "faithful Christian" things you can see, like showing up three times a week for church. Try to find someone within the Christian world who will argue that Christians as a group are doing well at the "hidden things," like personal Bible study, private prayer, and secret acts of compassion. By their pastors' own constant admonition, Christians have a "faith" that is defined by outward appearance, not inward maturity. Part of this has been caused by the culture war. Christians want people who show up at church, who publicly support a certain type of candidate (read: pro-life Republican), who boldly denounce evolution and humanism. All of those are expressions of *public faith*. In fact, Christian leaders have doubled down on this idea by repeatedly emphasizing the need to "stand up" for your faith in a hostile culture. It is not that these public expressions of faith are all intrinsically bad – some are positively essential. It is that divorced from a meaningful private faith and lived out in an environment that emphasizes appearing to be a good Christian, it is all too easy for these to become practices done for those around them to see.

To cite just one example: I recently saw a moving video of a Christian repeatedly approaching needy people in a grocery store offering to purchase their items as they were checking out. The people's responses were touching as many shed tears at the offer. The man then prayed with them or simply told them that the purchase was a gift from God. It was a beautiful idea, but here is the problem: they were *videotaping it*. Doing the act itself was apparently insufficient without lots of online hits to show off the action to the real audience: those around them.

The second illustration that Jesus gives in Matthew 23 of "everything they do is done for men to see" is also a *public faith* issue:

> "They love the place of honor at banquets and the chief seats in the synagogues."[12]

This discussion I will defer until my analysis of Luke 14 (our second "whoever exalts himself shall be humbled" passage), since that larger passage is almost completely focused on this idea, rather than only giving it a passing reference.

The third illustration in Matthew 23 of *public faith* centers on titles. Jesus critiqued the use of three titles:

> "they love to be greeted in the marketplaces and to have men call them 'Rabbi.' But you are not to be called 'Rabbi,' for you have only one Master and you are all brothers. And do not call anyone on earth 'father,' for you have one Father, and he is in heaven. Nor are you to be called 'teacher,' for you have one Teacher, the Christ."[13]

It is obvious how this would play into *public faith*. To be given honor and spiritual authority by these titles would easily set someone apart. The first term "Rabbi" would roughly translate over today into "pastor," "preacher," or "minister" within the Christian context. The second term ("Father") is likely not speaking of families, since the rest of the passage refers to religious titles, so we can presume that Jesus had in mind here someone considering himself to be a "spiritual father" to a newer believer. The third term has in mind someone guiding a newer believer in spiritual development (the NIV translates the term "teacher" while the NASB translates it "leader").[14]

The point in all three was how much the Pharisees liked being honored by people. They loved the respect that came with someone calling them "Rabbi" as they walked down the street. They loved the authority that was implied when a group of younger men called one of them their spiritual "Father." They loved when someone came up to them after synagogue and said, "Teacher, I have a question," knowing they were being looked to as the one with the answers. In the spiritual hierarchy, these titles were proof that they were at the top of the heap, admired by those around them. They loved and embraced this but not because they wanted to be used by God to touch people's lives. The passage began by telling us that "everything they do is done for men to see." They simply enjoyed the exaltation that came with those titles. The titles put them above those around them.

Do Christian leaders do this? Without question. It is not enough that they call themselves "Pastor" – they have to expand it to "Senior Pastor" (or "Lead Pastor" if you are in a church plant). It is a common saying for older pastors to call protégés their "sons in the ministry," which implies the "Father" moniker. Designating oneself as a "Teacher" is ubiquitous within Christian circles, including in some larger churches the title of "Teaching Pastor."

But what about the larger issue of exaltation by the titles? Here, the situation is actually worse. Standard conservative Christian theology gives lip service to "the priesthood of all believers," but the actual practice of their polity makes a sharp distinction between clergy and laity. The clergy are considered a class unto themselves. Church structures are such that great power and place is given to the clergy, with the laity expected to follow their lead. This remains consistently true across various approaches to church government. Even among the low church Baptists, who do not have bishops and put ultimate authority in each autonomous local congregation, the pastor still holds a disproportionate amount of authority.

Do clergy enjoy this arrangement? Again, without question. Just to cite one example, despite Jesus' words to the contrary on titles, they have fully embraced their ministerial designations without reservation. Considering so many Christian pastors speak consistently about the need to embrace the teaching of the whole Word of God, it is telling that this Matthew 23 "title" teaching is simply ignored. As one person has said, "The people like to put pastors on a pedestal, and the pastors like the view from up there."

What would be a better approach? Jesus shared it in the following verse: "The greatest among you will be your servant."[15] Rather than exalting themselves with impressive titles and then basking in the praise and respect they receive from those around them, Jesus called them to servanthood. Rather than taking the higher place, they instead were to be servants, like Jesus. Perhaps the most profound example of this was Jesus washing the disciples' feet at the Last Supper.

This, of course, seems counterintuitive: that your leaders would be servants. Is that not a recipe for disaster? How would that open up the door for God to move powerfully? The leaders being servants is actually exactly what Jesus wanted and it is absolutely essential for the church to see the power of God flow. How does that work? Well, the answer to that question is found in the final verse of this section of Matthew 23.

Whoever Exalts Himself Shall Be Humbled

We now examine the idea that forms the centerpiece of this book's chapter on the Pharisees' pride. This is the sentence that is the common denominator in the three passages we are studying. It is the concluding statement in this part of Matthew 23. Jesus taught:

> "Whoever exalts himself shall be humbled; and whoever humbles himself shall be exalted."[16]

What are we to make of this strange saying? Is this meaningless gibberish, like a sensei asking about the sound of one hand clapping? No, this is a fundamental spiritual principle that explains how to unleash the power of God in the Kingdom that Jesus inaugurated.

This is not incoherent rambling – this is practical advice to be followed.

What does that look like? We have studied the way that religious figures normally try to become exalted. They draw attention to how devoted they are to the teaching of God ("phylacteries wide," "tassels. . . long"). They pursue the places of honor. They readily embrace titles that let everyone know of their spiritual authority. In sum, they *exalt themselves*. (Or, to be slightly more generous, they accept the exaltation that those around them offer.) To go back to the first statement of this Matthew 23 section ("Everything they do is done for men to see"), the focus is on being *exalted* in the eyes of those around them.

When Christians behave in this way, Jesus has a promise for them: *they will be humbled*. That could mean that God simply does little or nothing spiritually powerful through their lives. That could mean that God allows their arrogance to have its ugly natural consequences. That could mean that God deliberately brings problems into their lives to teach them a much-needed lesson. Whatever way it happens, it is God's intent to bring humility into that life. "Whoever exalts himself shall be humbled."

On the other hand, when a Christian humbles herself, it sets her on a completely different path. It could be a willingness to take the least-wanted task at a church event. It could be doing acts of love within her neighborhood that no one knows about because they are behind the scenes and she does not write about it on Facebook. It could be the way she treats the janitors and service people at her workplace, even jumping in to help them when the opportunity presents itself. It could be the extra cup of coffee she buys for the homeless person she saw on her drive to McDonald's. Whatever the specifics of the situation, she is willing to be humble.

As she does this she lives her life in the same spirit Jesus did. Because she is willing to act this way, she begins to grow in spiritual maturity. She becomes more like Jesus. As that happens, she becomes someone through whom God can do greater things. The key for God being able to work through someone is her closeness to Christ – her spiritual maturity.

Now Jesus' positive promise comes to fulfillment: "whoever humbles himself shall be exalted." This does not mean that God necessarily gives her a lofty title and position, though that does sometimes happen. What it means is that she has become a person *through whom God can do great things*. She becomes "exalted" in spiritual power as she finds her life having a disproportionate impact on those around her. She finds that she often "just happens" to be in the right place at the right moment. She discovers that her words turn out to be exactly what that person needed to hear. She finds that the ministries in which she serves begin to see an outsized impact. She prays and sees her answers come more quickly and dramatically. Why is all this happening? Because God is working *through her*.

The heart of the teaching that Jesus gave here is the desire of God to move powerfully through His people. Jesus gave the key to seeing that happen. Do not grasp onto high position or jobs with impressive titles. That is the way the world finds its meaning. Instead, be willing to do the hidden things, the humble things, believing that as you do them you will gradually be transformed into a person through whom God can do great things. The problem of pride is not just that you live for the wrong audience ("Everything they do is done for men to see") but that it cuts you off from the path that will lead you to a spiritually powerful life.

Is the church today seeing God's power flow through it in mighty ways? Absolutely not. It is embarrassing how little evidence of the power of God most churches are seeing. Are Christian pastors today seeing God's power flow through them in mighty ways? Absolutely not. Instead, most are casting around attempting to find ways to manufacture ministry results.

Could it be that a major reason for this powerlessness is the pride of the church and its pastors? Could it be that they have exalted themselves and, in so doing, have cut themselves off from a primary source of God's power? Why are Christians known for being self-confident but not for being servants? Why are Christians known for pursuing political power but not for displaying God's power?

The Pharisees had a *public faith* that flowed from and fed into their pride. Christians also have a *public faith* that flows from and feeds into their pride. Many wonder why the church today is not seeing a powerful move of God within it. Could it come down to this:

"Whoever exalts himself shall be humbled; and whoever humbles himself shall be exalted."[17]

"Take the Lowest Place"

The second "exalts/humbled, humbles/exalted" passage is in Luke 14. Jesus was at a meal with a prominent Pharisee and He "noticed how the guests picked the places of honor at the table."[18] In response, He told a parable:

> "When someone invites you to a wedding feast, do not take the place of honor, for a person more distinguished than you may have been invited. If so, the host who invited both of you will come and say to you, 'Give this man your seat.' Then, humiliated, you will have to take the least important place. But when you are invited, take the lowest place, so that when your host comes, he will say to you, 'Friend, move up to a better place.' Then you will be honored in the presence of all your fellow guests."[19]

Jesus then added the tag line that is the recurring focus of this chapter:

> "For everyone who exalts himself will be humbled, and he who humbles himself will be exalted."[20]

I summarized the Matthew 23 passage in two words: *public faith*. For this passage, the two word summary is *social competition*. This takes us back to the elementary school cafeteria. If there are two open seats at your table and your "best friend" sits down next to

Matthew instead of next to you, there is an immediate reaction within you. "Why did he sit there? Does he like Matthew better than me?" We all feel deeply that social situations are usually "zero-sum games" – for one person to get a little higher, someone else is going to have to come down a few pegs. We are intrinsically social creatures and no one wants to be the one at the bottom of the totem pole. Because of that, we can be vicious in our relationships, all too willing to destroy someone else for the sake of our own social ascension. The world of relationships in which we live is a *social competition* and one that we want to win.

Into this environment comes Jesus' parable. Although the immediate context of His story is a wedding feast, it is easy to translate this into almost any social setting. It is, again, a "zero-sum game." If I am up front near the bride and groom, that speaks to my importance and prominence. It shows that "I am somebody." Conversely, if I sit at the back table near the waiters' entrance, it is visual proof that I have little standing. In Jesus' story, people were allowed to choose where they wanted to sit, so of course they chose the places of prominence. The place of pride within this battle is obvious.

Jesus gave advice that cut against the usual *social competition*. Rather than choosing the most impressive seat, instead "take the lowest place." He then gave two examples: a man in a place of honor is humiliated as the host tells him that seat is needed for a more distinguished guest, another man who did take the lowest place is approached by the host and is honored by being encouraged to move up to a better place.

At this point, we need to address something uncomfortable within the text. One generally presumes that Jesus told people to do the right thing simply because it was the right thing. What Jesus proposed here sounds a little like gaming the system. He did not tell people to "take the lowest place" just because that is what a humble person would do, but rather with the hope that you might be honored by being asked to move up higher. He did not tell people "do not take the place of honor" just because that is a prideful activity, but rather because you might end up humiliated before the whole crowd. What are we to do with this?

The big idea is that Jesus was trying to get prideful people to change their behavior. These are obviously spiritually immature people, since they are acting in this way. Perhaps mentioning the "real-life benefits" of pursuing His plan is a way to get them started in the right direction. After all, it is difficult for us to voluntarily give up social standing. A little incentive concerning the dangers and the benefits is the price to be paid to get some movement.

A similar practicality can be seen in the Golden Rule, which Jesus shared toward the end of the Sermon on the Mount. Jesus taught them:

> "In everything, therefore, treat people in the same way you want them to treat you, for this is the Law and the Prophets."[21]

The Golden Rule is so familiar that we rarely give its actual content much thought. Part of its intrinsic genius is that it turns our innate selfishness into something that works toward a good end. We all want to be treated well. We all want people to do what is right for us. Jesus took that innate selfishness and twisted it into something that helps us be more like God. "You know how you always want people to do right by you? Okay, make sure you do right by them in the same way too." This is practical life advice that not only works, but helps people to get started in obeying it. So, too, are the "real-life benefits" of Jesus' Luke 14 advice.

Having said all this to the crowd at the Pharisee's house, Jesus concluded His parable with these words:

> "For everyone who exalts himself will be humbled, and he who humbles himself will be exalted."[22]

What does this mean given the parable that precedes it? There are at least two levels of interpretation. One is the most obvious and straightforward. If you exalt yourself in social situations, you risk a humbling; if you humble yourself in social situations, you are opening the door to being exalted. The second level of interpretation goes along the same lines, but involves the activity of God. We can presume from these verses that God is actively working for the downfall of the social strivers while He also works to put those who are willing to take the "lowest place" into places of influence. (Again, this may be simply letting the consequences of their sin come to pass or at times might be an active movement by God.)

People are given the choice of having God working for them or against them. Jesus desired for His followers to put aside *social competition*, focus on pleasing God, and trust that He will work more powerfully through their humility to give them a more impactful life than their own efforts at social climbing could have manufactured.

Do Christians show any difference from the culture at large on the issue of *social competition*? None that is visible. They are every bit the strivers that the rest of society is. There is little reputation of Christians befriending the lowly and eschewing the powerful. Even among Christian pastors, how is it that they claim to be following the leading of the Spirit, yet that inevitably points them toward ever-larger congregations? The Spirit never wants pastors moving to smaller, less socially prestigious churches? Further, why is the American church so rigidly subdivided by class and race? Almost all congregations are homogeneous, with Christians "being led" to join churches that are uniformly people of their own race and their own socioeconomic class. Apparently the Spirit does not want them worshiping with anyone who is lower on the *social competition* ladder?

A small addendum: having said all this to the guests, Jesus then turned to the host and offered some related advice:

> "When you give a luncheon or dinner, do not invite your friends, your brothers or relatives, or your rich neighbors; if you do, they may invite you back and so you will be repaid. But when you give a banquet, invite the poor, the crippled, the lame, the blind, and you will be blessed. Although they cannot repay you, you will be repaid at the resurrection of the righteous."[23]

He first gave *social competition* advice for those attending gatherings; now He gives *social competition* advice for those hosting them.

The same rules normally apply: you want to have the most powerful, most influential, most cool, and most connected people at your gatherings. Your social standing rises when you are seen in the company of such people. Jesus gave advice that points in the opposite direction: invite the lowest on the social ladder. Presumably this is not intended to mean that Christians are never allowed to have a family gathering, but they should not be using their social gatherings to try to win the *social competition*.

The painful truth is that Christians ignore this passage. Sure, churches support soup kitchens, food pantries, and homeless shelters, but that is not really what this passage concerns. This is about Christians' private social activities. How many Christians have thrown a gathering and invited the least connected people they know? How often do Christians make it a point to go out to lunch with the most awkward person in their workplace? This simply does not happen with any regularity. Why? Because Christians are just as engaged in *social competition* as the rest of America. On this point, they have looked at Jesus' advice and decided they will try exalting themselves and see how that goes.

"God, I Thank You That I Am Not Like [Him]"

We now turn to the third passage where Jesus spoke His "exalts/humbled, humbles/exalted" truth. The first was Matthew 23's focus on *public faith*. The second was Luke 14's teaching on *social competition*. In Luke 18, the two-word summary for this story is *confident comparison*.

The context is religious people who felt superior to everyone else:

> To some who were confident of their own righteousness and looked down on everybody else, Jesus told this parable.[24]

These were religious people who felt smug in their personal holiness. Jesus' parable involves a Pharisee and a tax collector:

> "Two men went up to the temple to pray, one a Pharisee and the other a tax collector. The Pharisee stood up and prayed about himself: 'God, I thank you that I am not like other men – robbers, evildoers, adulterers – or even like this tax collector. I fast twice a week and give a tenth of all I get.'"[25]

It was an impressive list of religious activities from the Pharisee – and he had certainly impressed himself with what he had done. The tax collector, however, was not so confident:

> "But the tax collector stood at a distance. He would not even look up to heaven, but beat his breast and said, 'God, have mercy on me, a sinner.'"[26]

The tax collector made no claims to personal righteousness, but simply threw himself at the feet of God in hope of grace and mercy. Jesus then delivered the knockout punch:

> "I tell you that [the tax collector], rather than the [Pharisee], went home justified before God. For everyone who exalts himself will be humbled, and he who humbles himself will be exalted."[27]

The Pharisee had such an impressive moral resume to recommend him to God, but he was also filled with pride, which arose from his *confident comparison*. The Pharisee compared himself with the tax collector and felt pretty good. Jesus steadfastly rejected the Pharisee's analysis of his status. In truth, he was actually walking away from the temple with his sins still unforgiven because of his pride. Conversely, the tax collector essentially brought only his contrition and was absolved.

Here is a key truth to understand why Jesus said this: God does not judge humanity on a scale. Many people think as long as they are above average morally they will be okay before God. (And that becomes easier to achieve when you consider that we are pretty lenient in our evaluation of our own sinfulness.) In truth, though, God evaluates humanity by His perfect standard. This is why Christians believe that it was necessary for Jesus to die on the cross and be resurrected. Humanity could not earn its own salvation, but Jesus opened a spiritual door with His actions:

> "For God so loved the world, that He gave His only begotten Son, that whoever believes in Him shall not perish, but have eternal life."[28]

Therefore no one's good deeds are enough to earn his salvation:

> For it is by grace you have been saved, through faith – and this not from yourselves, it is the *gift of God – not by works*, so that no one can boast.[29]

A major part of the issue here is that *confident comparison* happens when people make that spiritual comparison *with those around them*. If they were to make that same comparison *with the perfection represented in Christ*, they would not feel quite as glib about their chances.

In this case, "everyone who humbles himself" refers to those who freely acknowledge their spiritual poverty and depravity and come to God knowing they have no reason for spiritual pride. Hat in hand, they hopefully confess their shortcomings and ask for mercy. They humble themselves. When that happens, God is pleased to "exalt" them. That includes a willingness to save those who ask.[30] It includes promising that those who receive Christ will become new spiritual creations.[31] It includes empowering those people with the Holy Spirit – God living within them.[32] It includes assurance of both abundant life on this earth and eternal life beyond this earth.[33]

Conversely, "everyone who exalts himself" refers to those whose spiritual pride blinds them to their true spiritual condition. This is not only those outside the church who feel as if they are good enough. It also includes many who sit comfortably week after week in the pews whose confidence is in their own goodness. They look at the world going to hell and they take comfort that they are "not like other men." They make their *confident comparison*. But these, like the Pharisee in the story, are rejected by God.

Christians have a problem with spiritual pride. They see themselves as the godly remnant within the United States. They are well known for their abrasiveness in their moral judgments, but not for their humility. They are renowned for being confident in the truth of their opinions, but not for their compassion. It is stunning how often their spiritual pride blinds them to the corrosiveness of their actions.

There are many contributing factors to Christians' pride: their love of increasingly fine dividing points in theology; their joyful arrogance in being right; their burden to stand for God against the "bad people" in society; the insufficient holiness (in their judgment) of those who disagree; the public's ignorance of the Bible leaving few with the knowledge to question Christians' viewpoints with Scriptural rebuttals.

In sum, Christians live in spiritual pride, believing that within American society, they are God's favorites because they are the righteous ones. They make *confident comparison* to those around them and are pleased to find themselves at the front of the line.

Pride and Powerlessness

The spiritual powerlessness of the church in America can be ably diagnosed by the centerpiece of this chapter:

> "For everyone who exalts himself will be humbled, and he who humbles himself will be exalted."

Christians maintain a *public faith* that seems to believe that what matters most spiritually is what is done "for men to see." Christians pursue *social competition*, attempting to climb the ladder rather than being willing to "take the lowest place." Christians find comfort in *confident comparison*, assured that they are performing so much better than those around them and thankful that they are "not like other men."

Instead of being exalted and empowered through God's movement, churches find themselves casting about to manufacture some evidence of progress. If the church were actually humble, it would find itself being exalted by God – used in powerful ways to make an obvious difference in the world. Its powerlessness is ample evidence of its pride problem. As stated earlier, there is an eminent practicality to this instruction that Jesus gives. It is not complicated. It is within reach. What will it take for Christians to humble themselves?

Chapter Three

"[They] Will Take Away Both Our Place and Our Nation"

Power, politics, and the culture war

The church decided to go all out for the Fourth of July service because the fourth actually fell on a Sunday that year. There were red, white, and blue banners across the front of the choir loft. The church's Boy Scout troop did the presentation of the colors, followed by everyone reciting the Pledge of Allegiance. Later in the service, the soloist sang a stirring rendition of Lee Greenwood's "God Bless the USA." The patriotism was soaring and the service was electric.

Finally, the preacher stood up for the morning sermon. "Turn with me in your Bibles to 2 Chronicles 7:14," he began. Before reading the verse, though, he silently walked out from behind the pulpit and down the stairs. His head bowed, he came to the front of the communion table before stopping and quietly standing for a moment, facing the congregation.

Without raising his head, he somberly said, "Our nation is in trouble." The congregation erupted with cries of "Amen." He looked up and repeated himself, "Our nation is in trouble."

He walked forward to the front of the aisle and continued, "This country began as a Christian nation. Our Founding Fathers believed in God and knew that America could not be great unless she was good!" The shouts of "Amen" from the congregation came louder with each sentence. "But today this country is not the one that they envisioned. We have seen the downward spiral of immorality and evil – those who take what is wrong and call it good – that have made this great country into a shadow of what it once was."

He put his hand on the front pew. "And those of us who sit each Sunday morning in a pew like this one? We're told that we don't have a place in this country. That our ways are too backward and that our time is past. We're told to sit down and shut up." He was shouting now. "But I say to you this morning that I will not be silent! America is a Christian nation and it is high time for God's people to stand up and reclaim what is rightfully ours! They have taken over and pushed us aside and you see the mess that we are in because of it. I say to you, it is time for God's people to rise up and reclaim the place that God intended them to occupy!" The congregation thundered back in approval.

He took his hand off the pew and pointed back to the pulpit. "How do I know this is God's will? Because I have a promise from God's Word! Let's look together at 2 Chronicles 7:14 and discover what God wants to see happen in the United States of America." With that, he turned to walk back to the pulpit, the congregation eager for the message to come.

The Pharisees' Loss of Power

One of the main reasons that the Pharisees were so vociferous in their opposition to Jesus was that He threatened their power. There is one point in the gospel of John where Jesus performed a great miracle that caused many people to believe in Him. The Pharisees fretted:

> "If we let Him go on like this, all men will believe in Him, and the Romans will come and *take away both our place and our nation*."[1]

They were worried that Jesus' gaining followers would mean that they would lose their power within that culture – both within the Jewish community and in relation to the Roman occupiers.

That statement is part of a section in the gospel of John that concentrates on the Pharisees' love of power (11:1 through 13:17).

Although there is enough interesting material to merit a book of its own, I will concentrate on the verses that highlight this chapter's theme of power. For the sake of clarity, I will number the major "power" statements in this part of John and handle them each in turn.

1. The raising of Lazarus.

The resurrection of Jesus' friend Lazarus and its immediate aftermath occupy all of John 11. From a literary standpoint, this is both the centerpiece and the high point of John's gospel. There are twenty-one chapters in John, so chapter eleven sits right at the center with ten before and ten after.[2] It is much more than just a number, though: this was the miracle that pushed Jesus' enemies to press their plans for His demise. It was a convincing sign to many who were there:

> Therefore *many* of the Jews . . . saw what He had done [and] believed in Him.[3]

These conversions pushed the Pharisees to fear Jesus' impact. There is a sense that John 11 begins the descent to the cross. For the purposes of this chapter, the best summary would be this: the raising of Lazarus was a public display by Jesus of His power and that demonstration left the Pharisees feeling that their power was threatened.

2. The Threatened Pharisees Plot Against Jesus.

Word of the many new believers caused by the resurrection of Lazarus quickly got back to "the chief priests and the Pharisees" who gathered to game plan a response:

> "What are we doing? For this man [Jesus] is performing many signs. If we let Him go on like this, all men will

believe in Him, and the Romans will come and *take away both our place and our nation.*"⁴

This is a crucial point: the Pharisees feared losing their power because of Jesus. When they said "our nation," they were referring to the possibility that Rome would end Israel as an entity and send the Jews off to other parts of the empire. When they said "our place," they were referring to the position of power they held within that nation – being religious leaders who were in charge within the limited independence that the Jews still held.

This certainly has a selfish element to it, but the Pharisees would have argued that was not their motive. Rather, in their mind, they were the remnant of Israel – the last of the Jews who took God's teaching seriously and deeply wanted to see the restoration of Israel to her former glory. To them, losing power meant Israel getting further from God. Therefore, in their minds, this would not have been an overt power play; it would have been doing what was best for the nation.

3. The Plot to Kill Lazarus.

The next section of John, which begins chapter 12, revolves around Jesus' being anointed in Bethany by Mary. The primary power issue here points us back to Lazarus and the Pharisees' unbelievable response to his resurrection:

> The large crowd of the Jews then learned that He was there; and they came, not for Jesus' sake only, but that they might also see Lazarus, whom He raised from the dead. *But the chief priests planned to put Lazarus to death also*; because on account of him many of the Jews were going away and were believing in Jesus.⁵

The chief priests, a group which included prominent Pharisees, responded to this threat to their power by deciding to kill the resurrected guy! Think of that: they did not change their mind even though someone being raised from the dead was obviously a powerful move of God; they did not embrace Jesus as someone through whom the power of God flowed; they did not celebrate the renewed life of Lazarus. Instead, they plotted to kill the person Jesus had resurrected.[6] The focus on preserving their own power so distorted their vision that they genuinely believed that was the best response to someone being raised from the dead.

This speaks loudly to the dangers of becoming deaf to reason and dumb to the movement of the Spirit when your heart is focused on preserving your power. Courses of actions that, if dispassionately considered, would be deemed absurd, suddenly seem viable and prudent. A place is quickly reached where anything is acceptable that removes the threat to your power.

4. The Triumphal Entry.

John 12 then moves directly into the Triumphal Entry of Christ into Jerusalem. Compared to what most would have expected for the arrival of the Messiah into Israel's capital, the actual event was surprisingly haphazard and spontaneous. The people heard that Jesus was on His way, cut palm branches, and spread the branches as well as their cloaks on the road.[7] Rather than arrive mounted high on a horse, the symbol of war, He instead rode a young donkey, a symbol of peace.[8]

Nonetheless, this spectacle further agitated the Pharisees. Lazarus continued to be a problem:

> So the people, who were with Him when He called Lazarus out of the tomb and raised him from the dead, continued to testify about Him. For this reason also the people went and met Him, because they heard that He had performed this sign.[9]

This miracle continued to threaten the Pharisees' power:

> So the Pharisees said to one another, "See, this is getting us nowhere. Look how *the whole world has gone after [Him]*!"[10]

You can hear the increasing desperation in their response.

5. The Question The Pharisees Won't Answer.

I am going to include here an interesting story that does not appear in John, but does appear in Matthew, Mark, and Luke shortly after the Triumphal Entry, so it is in the time frame we are examining – John just chose not to include it.[11] The religious leaders, who included many Pharisees, approached Jesus and inquired "by what authority" He was doing all His teaching and miracles.[12] Jesus replied with a question of His own:

> "I will ask you one question, and you answer Me, and then I will tell you by what authority I do these things. Was the baptism of John from heaven, or from men?"[13]

This put the religious leaders in a quandary, which they quickly realized:

> "If we say, 'From heaven,' He will say, 'Then why did you not believe him?' But shall we say, 'From men'?" – they were afraid of the people, for everyone considered John to have been a real prophet. Answering Jesus, they said, "We do not know."[14]

Their difficulty was this: John the Baptist had confirmed his belief in Jesus, so if they said that John was speaking on behalf of heaven, then Jesus would ask the Pharisees why they did not believe what heaven had said through John and believe in Him. That would short circuit their belief that He was a threat to their power and needed to be destroyed. If, on the other hand, they said that John the Baptist's works were "from men" (that is, not divinely inspired), they would raise the ire of the public:

> they were afraid of the people, for everyone considered John to have been a real prophet.[15]

I do not believe the statement that "they were afraid of the people" means that they were in fear of physical assault. I think it means that they were afraid of losing the support of the people for their religious authority, on which they based their beloved power. Not willing to lose that power, they passed on the question, telling Jesus that they did not know what the correct answer was.[16]

The importance for the larger point in this chapter is that there was a moment when they were forced to choose between publicly declaring their deeply held belief and clinging to their power. In that moment, they chose to hold to their power.

6. The Way of Sacrifice.

Now we turn to John 12:20-36 and an expression of how Jesus handled power. There was already a large Jewish crowd backing Him when a new constituency opened up:

> Now there were some Greeks among those who went up to worship at the Feast. They came to Philip . . . with a request. "Sir," they said, "we would like to see Jesus."[17]

At this critical moment Jesus even had non-Jewish people ("some Greeks") showing interest in Him and His message. This was a prime opportunity to further expand His base of followers; this was a prime opportunity for Him to expand His power.

Instead, He began to talk about sacrifice and death:

> "I tell you the truth, unless a kernel of wheat falls to the ground and dies, it remains only a single seed. But if it dies, it produces many seeds.... And I, if I am lifted up from the earth, will draw all men to Myself."[18]

Rather than looking to expand His power, He spoke of sacrificially dying to give life to others ("if it dies, it produces many seeds"). He acknowledged that He would be "lifted up" on the cross, but that this humble act of powerlessness would draw people to Him ("He was saying this to indicate the kind of death by which He was to die."[19])

This is a completely different view of power. It stands in stark contrast to the Pharisees' desperate grasping and duplicitous conniving. Jesus is not at all concerned about accumulating earthly power the way the Pharisees are. An exclamation point is put here with the final verse of this section. Having this throng of people eager to back Him, what did Jesus do?

> When [He] had finished speaking, Jesus left and hid [Himself] from them.[20]

First He had the passionate Jewish crowd at the Triumphal Entry calling Him the "King of Israel" and now there were even some Greeks interested in Him.[21] Jesus had crowds ready to give Him power and He walked away.[22]

7. The Motivation for Power Games.

The end of John 12 speaks of a mixed reaction to Jesus among the leaders:

> Nevertheless many even of the rulers believed in Him, but because of the

> Pharisees they were not confessing Him, for fear that they would be put out of the synagogue.[23]

The text goes on to inform us of an insightful detail concerning people and power:

> for they loved the approval of men rather than the approval of God.[24]

This provides an interesting coda to this series of sad statements concerning the Pharisees' power obsession. The Pharisees' hatred of Christ was largely born of their fear of losing power. Their clamor to retain that power led to a religious environment steeped in fear and silence, rather than love and honest inquiry. Those rulers who were on the fence knew what would happen to them if they were on the wrong side of this fight ("they would be put out of the synagogue") and they chose to retain the "approval" of the Pharisee leaders rather than stand with Jesus publicly. The obsession with power created a toxic religious environment for all involved.

8. Culmination: Jesus Washes the Disciples' Feet.

This series of power stories comes to its conclusion in the beginning of John 13 with an act of selflessness and servitude. With His disciples gathered for the Last Supper and the agony of the cross only hours away, Jesus did something that shocked those present:

> Jesus, knowing that the Father had given all things into His hands, and that He had come forth from God and was going back to God, got up from supper, and laid aside His garments; and taking a towel, He girded Himself. Then He poured water into the basin, and began to wash the disciples' feet and to wipe

> them with the towel with which He was girded.[25]

In that culture, the washing of feet was the job of a servant, yet Jesus was doing exactly that. Rather than demanding power, He was performing the act of the lowliest. Peter objected, but Jesus told Him that He was doing this to make a point about the nature of His followers when it came to power:

> "You call Me Teacher and Lord; and you are right, for so I am. If I then, the Lord and the Teacher, washed your feet, you also ought to wash one another's feet. For I gave you an example that you also should do as I did to you. Truly, truly, I say to you, a slave is not greater than his master, nor is one who is sent greater than the one who sent him."[26]

There have been arguments over the last two millennia whether Jesus literally meant for the washing of feet to be a regular activity in the church, but that is largely irrelevant to this discussion. After all these Pharisee power stories, we find Jesus commanding His followers to be servants, to take the lower job, to be focused on humble service rather than accumulating power. What a contrast. This is a call to lay aside the obsession with power and position and to be a servant.

In Luke's version of the Last Supper, Jesus told His disciples:

> "The kings of the Gentiles lord it over them . . . . But it is not this way with you, but the one who is the greatest among you must become like the youngest, and the leader like the servant . . . . I am among you as one who serves."[27]

A different paradigm to the usual power politics was being instituted along with the Eucharist.

So, to summarize the power passages in John 11-13, we are taught:

- Rather than being moved to belief by the resurrection of Lazarus, the Pharisees instead saw it as a threat to their place and nation,
- They responded, incredibly, by plotting to kill Lazarus,
- Their fears were heightened when the Triumphal Entry led them to conclude that the whole world had decided to follow Jesus,
- Jesus rejected the golden opportunity to consolidate His power after the Triumphal Entry and instead spoke of the need to sacrifice,
- Those in leadership who did believe in Jesus were unwilling to do so publicly because they desired the approval of the Pharisees, and
- Jesus gave the memorable example of washing the disciples' feet to teach that His Kingdom was to be one of kneeling to serve, not one of grasping for earthly power.

In sum, the Pharisees' passion for power plays prominently in their interactions with Jesus. In response, the hunger for power that the Pharisees repeatedly demonstrated was roundly rejected by Jesus and a new vision instituted.

"America Is a Christian Nation"

Do American Christians share the Pharisees' obsession with power? Without question. A majority of Christians' public persona over the last forty years has been centered in their pursuit of political power in an effort to "take our country back."[28] As that phrase suggests, there is a palpable sense among Christians that power they once held has been wrested from them, to the ill of country as well as Christians themselves. They desire to restore their power, with the fervent belief that their renewed power will mean a renewed America.

The history is pretty straightforward. The peak of church involvement in the U.S. was during the 1950s – an all-time high-water mark with 69 percent of Americans claiming church membership by the end of the decade.[29] Perhaps even more impressive, fully "80 percent of Americans believed the Bible was 'the revealed word of God.'"[30] The decline of church numbers since then, combined with the ongoing societal changes that conservative Christians find repulsive (to name the two greatest: the legalization of abortion and homosexual marriage) have left them feeling assaulted.

At the center of the battle to "take our country back" is the idea that America was founded as a Christian nation. This idea is the default opinion of conservative Christians on the subject, despite the glaring lack of evidence. There is plenty to be said about the historic arguments against understanding America as a Christian nation, but I will limit myself to the difficulties of this idea from a Biblical viewpoint. Having established those, I will turn to the unintended toxic outcome of the widespread acceptance of the "Christian nation" idea.

The Biblical argument is pretty straightforward: there are two "nations" the Bible speaks of as God's nations. In the Old Testament, that nation is Israel; in the New Testament, that nation is the church. In 1 Peter 2, we read concerning the church:

> But you are a chosen people, a royal priesthood, *a holy nation*, a people belonging to God.... Once you were not a people, but now you are the people of God.[31]

While it is certainly acceptable to state that secular nations have varying degrees of Christian influence, it is Biblically unacceptable to refer to any nations other than Israel and the church as nations of God. Therefore, in our present context, we could say that the church is a "Christian nation," but that cannot be said of America. We can say that America had Christian influences in its founding, but that is nothing like saying that it is a Christian nation.

This is not merely a matter of semantics. There is a monumental shift that has happened in Christians' interaction with the rest of society during the last forty years that finds its origin at this very point – the idea that America is a "Christian nation." This "Christian nation" assertion has lead to the culture war and the mess that has become of Christian witness.

Here is the basic outline of the standard evangelical argument: America was founded as a Christian nation; America is presently not anything approaching that; Christians are still standing nobly for the truth; therefore the problem is them. You know who I mean when I say "them." Conservative Christians blame the abortionists, the homosexuals, the liberals, the feminists, the Democrats, the secular humanists, the evolutionists, and the mainstream media. (That is not exhaustive, but it gets the big culprits.) The perennial drumbeat of conservative Christians fighting the culture war centers on the fact that the problem is "them" and America has to be won back. They endlessly quote the Old Testament passage 2 Chronicles 7:14:

> "If [My] people, which are called by [My] name, shall humble themselves, and pray, and seek [My] face, and turn from their wicked ways; then will I hear from heaven, and will forgive their sin, and will heal their land."[32]

This is God's promise, the evangelical argument goes, and it applies to America. The problem is "them" and their unwillingness to humble themselves, pray, and turn from their wicked ways. What is wrong with this country is "them."

The problem with that argument (and it is a massive problem) is that this promise is from the Old Testament. A solid argument could be made that it does not have a direct application today – that it was specific for Israel in that day and time or perhaps Israel throughout her ancient history. But if it does have direct application today, it would only be to *the nation of God*. That is not America, but the church. So if there is an application for today, it is not that *America* needs to repent in order to see God's forgiveness and healing, but that the *church* needs to repent to see God's forgiveness and healing.

This, of course, completely changes the dynamic of where blame is assigned. The problem is no longer "them;" for Christians, the problem is "us." After all, Christians believe it is impossible to live a righteous life without having been regenerated by the Holy Spirit. Why, then, should we be surprised that sinners are acting like sinners? The problem is not that sinners are acting like a bunch of sinners, but that the church is acting like a bunch of sinners.

This makes the culture war a completely misguided endeavor. Instead of assigning blame, Christians should be soul-searching. Instead of talking about how much God is displeased with Christians' culture war enemies, they should be sharing God's love and grace with them. Instead of trying to "win America back," they should be trying to get back to the heart of God.

The results of these mistakes are predictable. Christians have continued to live in a way that is distant from Jesus' commands. Christians have created deep wells of antagonism toward the very people they were supposed to be pointing to Christ. Christians have made no discernible progress in winning the "culture war" because it is a fight that God must find repugnant.

All of this, at its center, goes back to power. The motive for this effort was the belief among Christians that they were losing power within American society and something needed to be done to win it back. Their pursuit of power in this way has poisoned the well of God's love for a couple generations of Americans, who now associate Christians most strongly with being anti-homosexual and anti-abortion rather than being pro-grace and pro-mercy.

The John 11-13 passages shared earlier should be sufficient to provide an ongoing warning to Christians about the ugly end of the pursuit of power. Yet this clamor by Christians to regain power in America has gone almost entirely without dissent as to the wisdom of the pursuit. Instead, with each passing decade, ever more loudly has the cry gone out that greater zeal and harsher condemnation were fully justified in order to "win America back." Amid that clamor, it was nearly impossible to discern voices asking whether winning secular power was supposed to be the goal in the first place. Only now, decades in, has there begun to be a few rising voices asking if a tattered and soiled reputation for Christ's bride was a fair price to pay for a failed attempt to grasp political and social power.

I shared earlier that for many Christians the 1950s represent a magical time for "Christian America" – a time to which they deeply long to somehow return. The breathtaking thought of having almost three in four people claiming church membership is like a Siren song, enticing Christians to pursue whatever it takes to find a way to duplicate that time. It is worth noting that, for a country that was supposed to have been a "Christian nation" for nearly two centuries at that point, the history of American church membership is less than stellar:

> The percentage of Americans who claimed membership in a church had been fairly low across the nineteenth century, though it had slowly increased from *just 16 percent in 1850* to 36 percent in 1900. In the early decades of the twentieth century the percentages plateaued, remaining at 43 percent in both 1910 and 1920, then moving up slightly to 47 percent in 1930 and 49 percent in 1940.[33]

So much for a long history of being a God-fearing people.

The massive push in the 1950s to incorporate God into public life bore results in seeing more people in church.[34] This effort, with the help of Billy Graham and Dwight Eisenhower, pushed America toward that previously mentioned high-water mark of 69 percent of Americans claiming church membership.[35] That is less impressive, though, when one considers that during that time 47 percent of Americans "could not name even a single author of the gospels."[36] As Kevin Kruse writes in his excellent history of the era, "The American people, like Eisenhower, had become very fervent believers in a very vague religion."[37] I am reminded of the quote from an Anglican pastor who was asked about the size of his parish. He replied, "A mile wide and an inch deep."

Is this something to which it would be worth returning? Is getting as many people as possible into the pews a worthy goal if their faith is a bland cultural Christianity that bears little resemblance to the Bible's description of what it means to be a follower of Christ? Would Jesus be more pleased with a relative few passionate followers or with a massive majority of unchanged church members? (Eisenhower himself, long a believer in a vague non-denominational God, was baptized fewer than two weeks after his presidential inauguration and pressed to join a church. He chose the National Presbyterian Church in Washington, but quickly became frustrated at the pastor's lack of discretion. Ike told his press secretary, "You go and tell that goddam minister that if he gives out one more story about my religious faith I won't join his goddam church!"[38] This is the time for which conservative Christians long?)

America was not, is not, and cannot be a Christian nation. Christians' emphatically repeated claims to the contrary are historically ignorant and Biblically unfounded. Their desire to return there has more to do with the loss of cultural power than with a longing for an era of genuine Christlikeness.

The Moral Majority

One of the most famous and enduring phrases to come from the culture war is the moniker of Pastor Jerry Falwell's political machine. He called it "the Moral Majority." Falwell explained the name:

> "I was convinced that there was a moral majority out there among those more than 200 million Americans sufficient in number to turn back the flood tide of moral permissiveness, family breakdown and general capitulation to evil and to foreign policies such as Marxism-Leninism."[39]

This represented an important shift. Note that he was not attempting to influence those who would self-identify as evangelicals or even simply as Christians. He was pursuing a broader coalition that would include anyone who was in agreement with the idea that there was moral breakdown in society, that communism should be opposed, and that too often evil was having its way.

While there is nothing intrinsically wrong with attempting to gain political power by casting the net as widely as possible, there are substantial potential dangers when it is done by a minister in a manner that closely identifies the political effort with religious belief. One in particular is that people will shift from identifying Christianity as those who are making a concerted effort to be followers of Christ to those who generally agree with a few propositions about moral breakdown, communism, and evil in society. Such an endeavor would likely have the outcome of watering down the societal understanding of what it means to be a Christian. That, of course, is exactly what has happened over the last few decades.

The title "Moral Majority" speaks volumes. It is a name that would be chosen by someone pursuing power, not faithfulness to a way of life that requires sacrifice and self-denial. It is a name that presumes the building of a political coalition to acquire earthly influence. When Jesus spoke of His Kingdom, He said:

> "Enter through the *narrow* gate. For *wide* is the gate and *broad* is the road that leads to destruction, and *many* enter through it. But *small* is the gate and *narrow* the road that leads to life, and only a *few* find it."[40]

These verses envision the church, not as a "Moral Majority" ruling a country, but as a rebellion or a resistance movement. Christ's followers are working in enemy territory and their numbers are few, but they continue their brave fight to win as many to their cause as possible.

The tragic irony of the "Moral Majority" approach is that the Bible does speak of the followers of Christ being influential in society. The "small gate" statement occurred late in Jesus' Sermon on the Mount. Earlier in the Sermon on the Mount, Jesus said to His followers:

> "You are the salt of the earth . . . .
> You are the light of the world."[41]

This influence, though, was neither achieved by the accumulation of earthly power nor pursued in the hope of attaining earthly power. When before Pontius Pilate – the man who stated "Don't [You] realize I have the power either to free [You] or to crucify [You]?"[42] – Jesus pointedly declared,

> "My kingdom is not of this world. If My kingdom were of this world, then

> My servants would be fighting so that I would not be handed over to the Jews; but as it is, My kingdom is not of this realm."[43]

At the moment when Jesus had the most reason to exercise earthly authority (in order to save Himself from the cross), He instead flatly declared that was not the nature of the Kingdom He was inaugurating. Before this, when Peter tried to stop Jesus' arrest by wielding a sword, Jesus rebuked him:

> "Put your sword back into its place . . . . [D]o you think that I cannot appeal to My Father, and He will at once put at My disposal more than twelve legions of angels?"[44]

If He wanted to attain earthly power as normally understood, the means to make that happen were within His grasp. His mission, though, was not the accumulation of such power. We are given a clear picture of what His mission actually was in the verse that follows the most famous verse in the Bible:

> "For God so loved the world, that He gave His only begotten Son, that whoever believes in Him shall not perish, but have eternal life. *For God did not send the Son into the world to judge the world, but that the world might be saved through Him.*"[45]

The mission was not the accumulation of power; the mission was the redemption of people. One presumes that this would be accomplished in the spirit and with the humility of Jesus' washing the disciples' feet. It is a spirit that looks first to serve people, not lord it over them. It is a humility that takes the lesser seat rather than longing to be at the head of the table. It is an approach that is uniformly unconcerned with the accumulation of earthly power.

The Base Fear, The Base Passion

We see a focus on the regeneration and spiritual maturing of people in the Great Commission, which closes out Matthew's gospel:

> "Therefore go and make disciples . . .
> and teach . . . them to obey everything
> I have commanded you."[46]

What is especially interesting with regard to this chapter is the preceding verse. Jesus told His disciples:

> "*All power* is given unto [Me] in heaven and in earth."[47]

The power to complete the mission assigned was delegated to the disciples by Jesus. By extension, the church has the power from Christ to accomplish its given mission. This Christian pursuit of political power in the name of "taking America back" is not merely a misunderstanding of the mission that Christ gave the church; it is also a rebuke to Christ that whatever power He gave the church is not sufficient to do the job.

The focus of the church was not intended to be the accumulation of earthly power or the taking over of a secular nation. The mission given by Christ concerns the redemption of souls and instruction in the way of Christ that leads to abundant living. Certainly there are substantial ways that such an endeavor, properly pursued by the church and fully empowered by Christ, will impact the larger society. To the extent that improves culture and society, it is a welcome side effect. But it is exactly that: a side effect.

Christians' pursuit of a culture war represents a loss of vision of the mission that Christ gave the church. Christians' pursuit of a culture war has served to alienate the very people whom they were supposed to be winning. Further, Christians' pursuit of a culture war has failed on its own merits, failing to "take America back." This is undoubtedly because such a war was in no way empowered by Christ, who finds the whole endeavor misguided and counterproductive. We know this because of the extent to which the effort stands against the words He spoke.

The base fear that motivates this pursuit is the loss of power. The base passion that spurs this pursuit is the regaining of power. This, of course, is made more palatable by the refrain that Christians are winning America back *for God*. It is just a happy coincidence that getting America back for God also represents an increase in power, authority, and influence for Christians themselves.

The Pharisees of Jesus' day fretted that they would lose "both our place and our nation." Christians, in a manner so public as to be undeniable, have fought for the last few decades to regain their place and their nation. They have used non-Christian means in an attempt to achieve what they consider to be the Christian end of their resurgence to power. The evidence is ample that the outcome has been the same as in Jesus' day: "Jesus left and hid [Himself] from them."[48]

Chapter Four

"A People Who Will Produce Its Fruit"

Empty belief, a productive life, and a dead tree

Many years ago I received a phone call from a young woman about performing her wedding. I knew her but had never met her fiancé. We talked for a while and at one point in the conversation I asked if her fiancé was a Christian. She said he was not. We concluded the conversation without deciding anything.

A couple hours later she called me back. She had called her fiancé after our conversation and he said he was a Christian. He had been saved at a camp as a teenager.

I was struck by her comment (although I did not say anything in that moment). Here was someone speaking about the person with whom she was going to spend her life. Presumably they had talked for hundreds of hours about every imaginable subject as part of their dating relationship. Hopefully they knew each other better than they knew anyone else on earth. Yet when it came to the most important commitment a person can make in life, there had been no evidence in that fiancé's life that he was a Christian. In my initial conversation with the woman, she had no reason from his life to say that he was a Christian. There was no fruit in his life to point in that direction. Still, when directly asked, he was quick to say (and she to accept) that he was in fact a Christian because he had expressed a "belief" in Jesus many years before.

Some of you reading this are wondering why I was bothered by that. The answer concerns the importance of a life that is *spiritually fruitful*. Jesus claimed that the Pharisees were not producing godly fruit. He told the Pharisees that He was going to take away their spiritual authority and give His Kingdom to "a people who will *produce its fruit*."[1] He expected those claiming to be in the Kingdom of God to produce results that reflect the Kingdom of God. Further, He expected this new people to whom He intended to give the Kingdom to be *abundantly* fruitful. In one of the most important chapters in the gospels, He explained His vision of what His people would be like with a vineyard analogy:

> "I am the vine, you are the branches;
> he who abides in Me and I in him, he
> bears *much fruit*."[2]

In fact, He went so far as to claim that fruitfulness would be a defining characteristic of this new people:

> "My Father is glorified by this, that
> you *bear much fruit*, and so *prove to be My
> disciples*."[3]

"Fruit" is shorthand for what a life produces. Christians generally talk about two "types of fruit." One is internal fruit, which is a person becoming more like Christ. The best known passage on this is in Galatians 5:

> But the *fruit of the Spirit* is love, joy,
> peace, patience, kindness, goodness,
> faithfulness, gentleness, self-control.[4]

It is a Biblical expectation that a follower of Christ should become more like Jesus in his heart, mind, and soul. It is presumed that he will become more Christlike.

The second type is external fruit, which is the impact of a life in pointing people toward God. It might be witnessing and influencing someone to become a Christian. It might be sharing God's love by making a meal for the grieving family down the street. It might be leading your children to an accurate understanding of God through your daily walk with Christ. So, by "fruit" Christians mean the results of a life, both within a person as well as their impact on those around them.

A Lack of Fruitfulness

Jesus believed that the Pharisees were failing to produce godly fruit. Here are three passages that make that clear.

First, in Matthew 21, Jesus told the parable of the tenants.[5] A landowner planted a vineyard, rented it out to some farmers, and went away. At harvest time, the landowner sent back various representatives to collect his share of the vineyard's fruit. Rather than acknowledge the landowner's just and fair claim to fruit, the tenant farmers assaulted the representatives, even killing some. Finally, the landowner sent his son, but the tenant farmers killed him too. This was the point Jesus drew out of the story:

> "Therefore I tell you that the kingdom of God will be taken away from you and given to a people who will *produce its fruit*."[6]

The "you" in the parable were the tenant farmers and for Jesus they represented the chief priests and the Pharisees.[7] This "produce its fruit" comment is crucial: the reason the kingdom was being taken away from one group was that they were *not producing the desired fruit*.

The point was not lost on its intended audience. Two verses later the Bible says:

> When the chief priests and the Pharisees heard His parables, they understood that He was speaking about them.[8]

The passage makes it abundantly clear that Jesus was dissatisfied with the Pharisees because they were not producing the fruit that should come with being God's people.

Second, in Luke 13, Jesus told a different story:

> "A man had a fig tree, planted in his vineyard, and he went to *look for fruit* on it, but did not find any. So he said to the man who took care of the vineyard, 'For three years now I've been coming to *look for fruit* on this fig tree and haven't found any. *Cut it down!* Why should it use up the soil?' 'Sir,' the man replied, 'leave it alone for one more year, and I'll dig around it and fertilize it. *If it bears fruit next year, fine!* If not, then *cut it down.*'"⁹

The clear implication of the story is that *the master expects fruit*. Yes, he had some patience and was willing to give a little more time, but that patience was not endless. The passage is equally clear that a lack of fruitfulness would eventually lead to judgment ("cut it down").

John the Baptist shared a similar sentiment:

> "The ax is already at the root of the trees, and every tree that *does not produce good fruit* will be cut down and thrown into the fire."¹⁰

In both passages, it is clear that failing to bear fruit results in judgment. Fruitfulness is expected, not optional.

A third passage concerns a peculiar incident where Jesus killed a fig tree. This is a bit more complicated and therefore requires more explanation. In Mark 11, Jesus traveled from Bethany to Jerusalem:

> On the next day, when they had left Bethany, He became hungry. Seeing at a distance a *fig tree* in leaf, He went to see if perhaps He would find anything on it; and when He came to it, He found *nothing but leaves*.... He said to it, "*May no one ever eat fruit* from you

again!" And His disciples were listening.[11]

Jesus' words had impact, as evidenced the following day[12]:

> As they were passing by in the morning, they saw the *fig tree withered from the roots up*. Being reminded, Peter said to Him, "Rabbi, look, *the fig tree* which You cursed *has withered*."[13]

This raises eyebrows: why did Jesus curse the fig tree?[14] Was He having a bad day? Did He have anger issues? Was He trying to show off His power? No – none of those is the answer. Rather, the reason becomes obvious when we look at the larger Biblical context.

There are several places in the gospel of Mark where the author used what some call "sandwiches." A regular sandwich is bread, then meat (or peanut butter or whatever), then bread. Mark wrote some of his stories in the same way: he started on a story (bread), then shifted to another subject (meat), then came back to that first story (bread again).[15] In those cases, the "outside" parts and the "inside" part are always intimately connected and are clearly meant to be interpreted in light of each other. That is true for this passage as well. The "bread" of this passage is the fig tree. The first slice is Jesus cursing the fig tree; the second slice is the fig tree being found withered the next morning.

So what is the "meat"? Here it is:

> Then they came to Jerusalem. And He entered the *temple* and began to drive out those who were buying and selling in the *temple*, and overturned the tables of the money changers and the seats of those who were selling doves; and He would not permit anyone to carry merchandise through the *temple*. And He began to teach and say to them, "Is it not written, '*My house shall be called a house of prayer for all the nations*'?

> But you have made it a *robbers' den*."
> The chief priests and the scribes heard this, and began seeking how to destroy Him.[16]

The "meat," or "inside" of the story, is Jesus' expressing physically and verbally His great displeasure with what the temple system had become. God's house was supposed to be a "house of prayer for all the nations" but it had been transformed into a "robbers' den." The Pharisees, well represented among the mentioned "chief priests" and "scribes," were not producing godly fruit.

Suddenly, the fig tree story that precedes and follows this temple incident makes sense. Why did Jesus curse the fig tree? "He found nothing but leaves" – that is, *no fruit*. Jesus' decision to curse the fruitless fig tree was a symbol of His rejection of the fruitless temple system. In many ways, the temple system was both physically and psychologically the centerpiece of the Pharisees' religion. Jesus, however, found the beehive of activity failing to produce the servants of God that the Father desired. It was not producing the *fruit* that God desired. The fig tree is a picture of Jesus' intention to put aside the Old Testament temple system and inaugurate something new, which the Bible teaches is new life through Jesus' death and resurrection and the advent of the church as His people.

This dramatic sign again points to Jesus' expectation of fruitfulness. The fruitless fig tree is symbolic of the fruitless temple system that the Pharisees so idolized. Jesus destroyed the fruitless tree and the fruitless temple system.

In sum, looking at all three passages, the point is clear: Jesus repeatedly condemned the Pharisees for their lack of godly fruit.

Are Christians Bearing Godly Fruit?

Like the Pharisees, are American Christians failing to bear godly fruit? The answer is a definitive "yes"; and, sadly, proving it is fairly easy. I will share four arguments.

First, a major Christian study found that more than 80 percent of born-again Christians, individuals who believe that salvation has been extended to them through a personal salvation experience with Jesus, believe that a valid definition of "spiritual maturity" is "trying hard to follow the rules." This was true even though those same people believed that "salvation is not earned through 'good works'."[17] That is the exact approach the Pharisees took – follow all the rules. (This is crucial – more on this in a moment.) So most believers define valid faith in the same, fruitless way the Pharisees did.

Second, the perceptions of those outside the church give some indication whether Christians are living fruitful lives. The news is, unsurprisingly, not good. One study asked opinions of young people who do not go to church. "Nearly nine out of ten young outsiders (87 percent) said that the term *judgmental* accurately describes present-day Christianity. This was one of the big three – the three most widely held negative perceptions of Christians (along with being antihomosexual and hypocritical)."[18] Equally sad, only 15 percent of those young non-Christians "thought the lifestyles of those Christ followers were significantly different than the norm."[19] Of course, public perception is not necessarily the same as reality, but here the numbers are significant because they point in the same direction as the other three points I am sharing.

Third, many American Christians talk prominently about "taking our country back" and "returning America to Biblical values." Both of these ideas are problematic (issues already discussed earlier in this book), but for the moment we will simply take them at face value. Christians solemnly proclaim that America continues a "moral slide" away from Biblical values. The people who could most obviously make a difference in turning things around would be those in the church. (After all, Christians believe that the Bible teaches that it is impossible for non-Christians to live a godly life until they have first experienced salvation through Christ.) If the church were actually being "salt" and "light" as they are called to be by Jesus, would there not be some reversal of the perceived downward spiral?[20] Are Christians' perpetual complaints about the immorality of America not in fact an indictment of their own lack of impact and fruitfulness?

Finally, a recent survey found that 52 percent of American Christian adults believe that their church "definitely does a good job helping people grow spiritually." An additional 40 percent believe that it "probably" does so. That is a supermajority of 92 percent of

American Christian adults who believe their church is doing a good job growing them spiritually toward fruitfulness. Do American church leaders agree with that assessment? In the same survey, those leaders were asked if they believe modern American churches are "doing very well" or "somewhat well" at "discipling new and young believers." Nearly two-thirds of pastors answered in the affirmative.[21] Not quite as high as the people in the pews, but still a high number.

The dismal numbers on spiritual maturity and fruitfulness contained in this section leads one to believe that both the congregations and clergy have lost a vision for what Biblical fruitfulness looks like. These numbers point toward an American Christian population that is content with what they are receiving because they have no notion of anything higher. This is substantiated by a separate survey that showed that half of American church attendees were "unable to venture a guess" regarding how their church would define a "healthy, spiritually mature follower of Jesus." The researchers concluded "many churchgoers and clergy struggle to articulate a basic understanding of spiritual maturity. People aspire to be spiritually mature, but they do not know what it means."[22] The other numbers shared in this section make it clear that Christians are not living in a way that is bearing the fruit of the gospel, yet the Christians in the pews seem content with what their church is offering. They have, like the Pharisees, come to accept something inadequate as being normative.

The Dividing Line

Why did the Pharisees so completely lack godly fruit? To find the answer, it is essential to understand what the Pharisees saw as the spiritual dividing line between those who were in and those who were out. The dividing line for them was belief in and obedience to the rules.

It is well known that they had developed many additional rules in order to "help people" better follow the Old Testament Law. For them, the rules included not only the original Mosaic Law, but also all of their "add ons." The rules became an end to themselves and the focus of their faith.

Southern Baptist scholar A.T. Robertson wrote that the Pharisees put "the oral law [their additional rules] on a par with the Old Testament Scriptures."[23] He quoted ancient writer Josephus in making his point:

> "What I would now explain is this, that the Pharisees have delivered to the people a great many observances by succession from their father, which are not written in the laws of Moses."[24]

This love of rules was colorfully conveyed by Jesus when He said that the Pharisees

> "tie up heavy loads and put them on men's shoulders, but they themselves are not willing to lift a finger to move them."[25]

Trying to faithfully follow the manifold rules was indeed a "heavy load."

Robertson shared some of the ridiculous minutiae to which the Pharisees' laws could descend:

> One was not allowed to write on the Sabbath, save on something dark or with the hand upside down. One was not allowed to read by lamplight or to cleanse clothing. Women were not to look in the mirror on the Sabbath day because they might see a grey hair and be tempted to pull it out. Some knots could be tied on the Sabbath and others not . . . . Vinegar could be used for a sore throat if it was swallowed, but not as a gargle . . . . An egg laid on the Sabbath day could be eaten,

> provided one intended to kill the hen.²⁶

A prime example of this obsessive focus on the rules happened in Matthew 12 and surrounded a healing Jesus performed on the Sabbath:

> Departing from there, He went into their synagogue. And a man was there whose hand was withered. And they questioned Jesus, asking, "*Is it lawful to heal on the Sabbath?*" – so that they might accuse Him.²⁷

Notice their question: is it *lawful* to heal on the Sabbath? Their focus was on their rule, which was that such a healing would constitute work and therefore was banned on the Sabbath day of rest. Within this, of course, there was no thought for the man with the withered hand.

Jesus replied to them:

> "What man is there among you who has a sheep, and if it falls into a pit on the Sabbath, will he not take hold of it and lift it out? How much more valuable then is a man than a sheep! So then, it is *lawful to do good on the Sabbath.*"²⁸

Jesus directly rejected their theology's excessive focus on rules. He healed the man despite the Pharisees' objections. This cut so deeply into the Pharisees' spiritual identity that their response is shocking:

> But the Pharisees went out and conspired against Him, as to how they might destroy Him.²⁹

"Destroy" means they wanted to kill Him.

Think of that: the Pharisees' focus was so intent on believing and obeying their rules that Jesus flagrantly disobeying a rule led their minds to believe that He deserved to be *killed*. Not rebuked, not chastised, not sent a strongly worded letter. Killed! That was their dividing line and Jesus crossed it.

In sum, the Pharisees were focused on belief in and obedience to their rules and in so doing completely failed to produce the fruitfulness God desired.

Christian Belief and Obedience

Having established the approach of the Pharisees, we now turn our attention to consider whether American Christians are in a similar situation. There are two different approaches among Christians to belief and obedience, but both lead to a lack of godly fruitfulness.

The first approach can be characterized as being found among many conservative Christians. This is a legalistic approach to the Christian faith and involves a lengthy list of mandatory (although usually unwritten) rules that members of the congregation are expected to follow. These rules could include things like attendance at three services a week, participating in a small group Bible study each week, listening only to contemporary Christian music, using a particular version of the Bible (like the ESV), voting Republican, strong support for Israel, contemporary music in worship, denial of evolution, a certain style of preaching (usually expository) as well as rules specific to individual churches.

It figures even more prominently among those who self-identify as "fundamentalists." These rules usually include things like attendance at three services a week, not smoking, homeschooling or Christian school for children, refusing vaccinations, only using the King James Version of the Bible, not dining at restaurants that serve alcohol, not dating, denial of evolution, a certain style of preaching (often involving yelling), not celebrating Halloween, strong support for Israel, not ordaining women, spanking as a form of child discipline, no drums or electric guitars in worship, and only singing hymns. The variety of potential additional items on this list is great since there are so many types of fundamentalists.

I am not arguing that all the items on these lists are intrinsically bad, but there are twin problems with this approach. The first problem is that the list often includes items that are not specifically Biblical, yet get lifted to the level of mandatory. Just to cite one of the above examples, nowhere in the Bible does it say that you have to vote Republican, yet that is considered a non-negotiable part of being a faithful Christian within many churches. What is the impact of that belief? The parts of the Bible that agree with the Republican agenda are emphasized (like pro-life ideas) while the parts that disagree are ignored or diminished (like compassion for the poor). Additionally, the name of God is invoked publicly on behalf of things that He never endorsed (for example, Christian organizations supporting the repeal of the estate tax because that is a Republican priority).

The second problem is that this approach limits the scope of obedience. Rather than the Christian walk being one where you have to follow Jesus in all aspects of your life, instead you just have to follow the limited rules on which the congregation focuses. To cite one example, Jesus talked a lot about the dangers of money, yet in many rule-focused congregations the only admonition spoken concerning money is that you should tithe. There is no rebuke of the materialistic passions of American society or critique of the celebration of greed within capitalistic economies. Those are not in the rules, so as long as you are tithing you can do whatever you want with the rest of your money. By contrast, when a Christian understands that Jesus is Lord over his *whole life*, it means that every part of his life is subject to direction and change from Him. That is a much more challenging proposition.

This rules-based approach to Christianity almost always leads to churches who are strongly convinced of their own correctness (and the corresponding wrongness of most other churches). It also leads to a strict, repressive faith. What it almost never leads to is the abundant fruitfulness that Jesus pointed toward as being the natural result of being His follower. These churches are not known for their overflowing mercy and love. (That may be the understatement of the year.) They are proudly known for their "faithfulness" to the "truth" as they perceive it. As with the Pharisees, we see a focus on belief in and obedience to a set of rules that fails to produce a godly fruitfulness.

The second approach to fruitfulness among Christians focuses on one item rather than a whole list. The focus is on saying that you "believe in Jesus." Christians have dumbed down "believe in Jesus" to where it only means "mentally agree with the idea that Jesus existed." That means when you ask someone if they "believe in Jesus," their affirmative answer means "Yes, I believe that Jesus lived 2,000 years ago, died on a cross, and was resurrected from the dead." They believe that *as a fact*. When the Bible speaks of "believing in Jesus," it has in mind the idea of someone believing that Jesus lived, died, and was resurrected, but also that He was who He claimed to be and that we are to be followers of His teaching. We are to believe *as an act of obedience*.

There is an old story of a tightrope walker preparing to go across Niagara Falls. He brought a wheelbarrow out before the crowd and asked, "Who thinks I can push this wheelbarrow across the tightrope?" The crowd roared its confidence. "Who thinks I can push this wheelbarrow across the tightrope with a person in it?" The crowd roared its confidence. Then he said, "Great! Now, who will get in the wheelbarrow?" And the crowd was silent. Belief is not saying you think Jesus can do it; belief is getting in the wheelbarrow. Belief is not saying you think Jesus is great; belief is actually obeying the teaching of Jesus.

Some will object that the Bible says that you only have to believe:

> if you confess with your mouth Jesus as Lord, and *believe* in your heart that God raised Him from the dead, you will be saved.[30]

That verse certainly contains an important Biblical truth. Again, though, it is important to remember what "believe" means. Consider the words of Jesus:

> "Not everyone who says to Me, 'Lord, Lord,' will enter the kingdom of heaven, but he who *does the will of My Father* who is in heaven."[31]

A clear picture emerges when these two ideas are taken together. Yes, it is necessary to "believe in Jesus," but that belief includes acknowledging His claims on your life. He called His people to "follow Me," which means taking His teaching seriously by attempting to live those truths out.[32] He expects you to pursue the will of God in your life.

This empty "belief" approach leads to fruitlessness. There are millions of American Christians who say they "believe in Jesus" yet make little or no attempt to actually experience the abundant life that Jesus offered. They make no effort to live out Jesus' teaching. Because of that, their lives are inevitably devoid of spiritual fruit. And, tellingly, that fruitlessness does not bother them because they firmly think that all they need is their stated belief in Jesus.

Jesus' Vision of a Fruitful People

Having analyzed the fruitfulness shortcomings of the Pharisees and Christians, for the second half of this chapter we turn to casting a positive vision. What did Jesus' teachings portray as the normative life of a follower of Christ regarding fruitfulness?

First, we will look at Jesus' understanding of fruitfulness. Did Jesus believe fruitfulness was necessary or a nice bonus? Did Jesus believe fruitfulness would be hidden or obvious? Did Jesus believe fruitfulness would be marginal or abundant?

Second, we will examine Jesus' primary teaching on the practical path to actually bearing fruit.

Is Fruitfulness Necessary Or a Nice Bonus?

There are a multitude of passages that indicate for Jesus fruitfulness was not a nice bonus, but rather a necessary and expected part of the normal life of a follower of Christ. By "necessary," I am not arguing that Christians are saved by works, but simply that fruitfulness is a natural consequence of living as Jesus intended. A few examples:

1. **Having no fruit leads to being "cut off" or "thrown in the fire."**

Consider this passage from Luke 13 that we looked at earlier. Read it again with closer attention to Jesus' words about the judgment that a lack of fruit brings:

> "A man had a fig tree, planted in his vineyard, and he went to *look for fruit* on it, but did not find any. So he said to the man who took care of the vineyard, 'For three years now I've been coming to *look for fruit* on this fig tree and haven't found any. *Cut it down!* Why should it use up the soil?' 'Sir,' the man replied, 'leave it alone for one more year, and I'll dig around it and fertilize it. *If it bears fruit next year, fine!* If not, then *cut it down.*'"[33]

The clear implication of the story is that the master *expected* fruit. He is willing to allow for some extra time, but that patience is not without limit. The failure to bear fruit will lead to it being cut down.

In the Sermon on the Mount, Jesus spoke of fruit as a way to divide the people of God from God's enemies:

> "Watch out for false prophets. They come to you in sheep's clothing, but inwardly they are ferocious wolves. By their fruit you will recognize them. Do people pick grapes from thornbushes, or figs from thistles? Likewise every good tree bears good fruit, but a bad tree bears bad fruit. A good tree cannot bear bad fruit and a bad tree cannot bear good fruit. *Every tree that does not bear good fruit is cut down and thrown into the fire.* Thus, by their fruit you will recognize them."[34]

Those who do not have "good fruit" are "cut down and thrown into the fire."

John the Baptist shared a similar sentiment in a verse we referenced earlier:

> "The ax is already at the root of the trees, and every tree that does not produce good fruit will be *cut down and thrown into the fire.*"[35]

There is a famous passage that the Apostle Paul wrote that initially seems to point in another direction, but actually fits perfectly with this point. Speaking in 1 Corinthians about the future judgment of Christians, Paul wrote:

> For no man can lay a foundation other than the one which is laid, which is Jesus Christ. Now if any man builds on the foundation with gold, silver, precious stones, wood, hay, straw, each man's work will become evident; for the day will show it because it is to be revealed with fire, and the fire itself will test the quality of each man's work. If any man's work is burned up, he will suffer loss; but he himself will be saved, yet so as through fire.[36]

Some points of initial explanation: the "work" talked about here is a person's life work; the "fire" is the judgment of God.

The image of being "saved, yet so as through fire" is a well-known one in Christian circles: it is preached as referring to the "lukewarm" or half-hearted believer who makes it to heaven but does so empty-handed (he has done no works for Christ during his life, spiritually speaking). He therefore receives little or no rewards or praise from Christ. The standard Christian thought on this matter is that this is evidence that you can believe the right things but not live a spiritually productive life. Having lived a life where you believed in Jesus but did not do anything for God, you still are "saved," but having done no works for Him and therefore having nothing to show for your life means that you come into heaven "as through fire" (similar to fleeing a burning house through the flames, taking nothing with you as you run but getting out alive yourself). Again, though, the right belief is the proof that you are a real believer, even in the presence of no fruit in your life.

That line of thinking represents a misunderstanding of this passage. The crucial point is this: both types of people mentioned had "work" to be tested. Both had produced something. They were not empty-handed as they came into judgment. This judgment tested the *quality* of the work, not whether the person had any work.[37] To use the key word in this chapter, the judgment tested the quality of the *fruit*, not whether the person had any *fruit*.

So this passage also points in the direction of every true follower of Christ producing fruit. Fruitfulness is necessary, not exceptional.

2. Jesus gave the kingdom to someone new who would produce its fruit.

A second proof returns to Matthew 21 and the parable of the tenants. As you may recall from earlier in the chapter, the landowner rented his vineyard, but when harvest time came the tenant farmers refused to give the landowner the fruit that he deserved. They beat up the representatives he sent, even eventually killing the landowner's son. This was the point Jesus drew out of the story:

> "Therefore I tell you that the kingdom of God will be taken away from you and given to a people who will *produce its fruit*."[38]

The point is not lost on its intended audience. A couple verses later the Bible says:

> When the chief priests and the Pharisees heard His parables, they

> understood that He was speaking about them.[39]

The passage makes it abundantly clear that Jesus was dissatisfied with the Pharisees because they were not producing the fruit that should come with being God's people. Jesus gave His kingdom to a new group of people who would produce the fruit of the kingdom in their lives. This is not a side issue, but is the stated reason for the transfer. It shows that fruitfulness is a major expected result for the new system, not a nice extra.

3. Producing fruit is so essential that Jesus can use it to separate believers and non-believers.

Here we find a famous passage that does not easily fit into traditional Christian theology. Even many non-Christians are familiar with Jesus' words that:

> "whatever you did for one of the least of these . . . you did for [Me]."[40]

The idea is that when we help the lowest of people, in doing that we are helping Jesus.

The Matthew 25 story actually begins with Jesus talking about Final Judgment:

> "But when the Son of Man comes in His glory, and all the angels with Him, then He will sit on His glorious throne. All the nations will be gathered before Him; and He will separate them from one another, as the shepherd separates the sheep from the goats."[41]

The "Son of Man" is one of many titles that the Bible uses for Jesus, so the picture here is of Jesus judging everyone at Final Judgment. The "sheep" are the righteous; the "goats" are the unrighteous.

Here is the tricky part: what does this passage tell us about the criteria for separating the sheep from the goats? This is what Jesus said to the "sheep":

> "Then the King will say to those on His right, 'Come, you who are blessed of My Father, inherit the kingdom prepared for you from the foundation of the world. For I was hungry, and you gave Me something to eat; I was thirsty, and you gave Me something to drink; I was a stranger, and you invited Me in; naked, and you clothed Me; I was sick, and you visited Me; I was in prison, and you came to Me.'"[42]

The righteous ask when they did any of those things to Him and He responds that

> "whatever you did for one of the least of these . . . you did for [Me]."[43]

To pick one example from the list, when you invite a hungry homeless person to lunch, Jesus sees that as though you had invited Him to lunch.

The passage continues with Jesus now addressing the "goats." Essentially the same conversation happens, but this time the "goats" did not do anything for those who are "the least of these" and therefore judgment falls:

> "He will reply, 'I tell you the truth, whatever you did not do for one of the least of these, you did not do for [Me].' Then they will go away to eternal punishment, but the righteous to eternal life."[44]

If this passage were just a generic "be nice to struggling people" encouragement, then there would be no issue here, but this passage represents a challenge for Christian theology. Why? Because Christians consistently preach that salvation comes through grace by faith in Jesus and that having such belief in Jesus is the difference between those who are saved and those who are lost. Given that, though, we should expect this passage on Jesus separating the sheep (the righteous; the Christians) from the goats (the unrighteous; the non-believers) to involve Jesus asking each person what their belief is or if they have faith in Him. *But that is not what it says.* The judgment is not based on their words, but their actions. To use the word this chapter is focusing on, He focused on whether their life bore *fruit* – the hungry fed, the stranger welcomed, the prisoner visited.

That is the basis of Jesus' judgment. *That* is the criteria He used to separate the "sheep" and the "goats." By the standards of mainstream Christian thought, that is absolutely the wrong criteria. To separate the saved from the unsaved, Jesus should have asked, "What do you believe?"

Now, what are we to do with this? I would propose this would be the best (and most Biblical) approach for Christians: godly fruit is a *defining characteristic* of the life of a true follower of Jesus and if you do not have that fruit then you are *by definition not a follower of Jesus*. Because fruit is a defining characteristic, Jesus can judge them based on their fruitfulness of their lives. Christians *by Biblical definition* act like this, therefore if you do not act like this there is abundant reason to question the integrity of your profession of faith.

To put it another way: if you do not do the things enumerated on that "sheep" and "goat" list, you are not a follower of Jesus, no matter how thick your Bible, how staunchly traditional your theology, how old your church, how celebrated your presence in your congregation.

When you add up these three points, it is abundantly clear that God expects fruit. Christians have attempted to redefine true belief in terms of correct theology, making fruitfulness a nice bonus for an exceptional few. Instead, Biblically, fruitfulness is a defining characteristic of a true follower of Christ.

Is Fruitfulness Hidden Or Obvious?

A thought that follows the above idea that fruitfulness is necessary is whether such fruitfulness is hidden or obvious. That is, if fruitfulness is a characteristic of the follower of Christ, could it not be true that usually such fruitfulness would be so hidden as to be essentially invisible? Jesus answered that question definitively. He stated that a Jesus tree produces Jesus fruit. He taught that fruitfulness is not hidden, but obvious. Earlier in this chapter was a portion of Jesus' Sermon on the Mount. Allow me to quote it again, but this time focusing on a different truth within it:

> "Watch out for false prophets. They come to you in sheep's clothing, but inwardly they are ferocious wolves. *By their fruit you will recognize them.* Do people pick grapes from thornbushes, or figs from thistles? Likewise every *good tree bears good fruit*, but a *bad tree bears bad fruit*. A good tree cannot bear *bad fruit* and a bad tree cannot bear *good fruit*."[45]

I want to focus on the last two sentences. Jesus said that a "good tree bears good fruit" and a "bad tree bears bad fruit." He then doubled-down by stating the negative that a "good tree cannot bear bad fruit" and a "bad tree cannot bear good fruit." This is a difficult saying. We tend to presume that all lives are a mix of good and bad, but Jesus pointed us in another direction.

I will try to give some help in understanding that in a minute, but first let me make the main point. In spite of Christians regularly saying things like "There is no way to know whether you are having an impact or not" or "We will not know until we reach eternity if we have done any good," this passage points in the opposite direction. It states that fruitfulness is clear and obvious. Certainly there are some situations where a person will not know in this life whether they had an impact, but that does not change the overall truth here. A good tree produces good fruit.

Why do Christians not preach this? Because they have dumbed down "belief" to merely mean verbal assent to a list of doctrines. There is no expectation in most Christian circles that *the normal Christian life* will bear obvious fruit. There may be a hope that it will happen for the particularly good Christians, but it is seldom stated that fruitfulness is *normative for the Christian life*. While Christians rightly claim the Biblical truth that salvation comes by grace through faith, they also need to proclaim the Biblical truth that such a powerful salvation produces a clear change in a person's life. We are not saved by works, but when we are truly saved there will be evidence in our lives that the most powerful Being in the universe has taken up residence within us.

Now, how can Jesus have made such bold statements here – would it not be truer to say every life is a mixed bag? I certainly invite Christians to come up with better explanations than this (since they believe the Bible is the Word of God so these verses have to be accepted as truth), but I will share two thoughts that are somewhat helpful to me in understanding this.

First, concerning the good bearing good fruit, I think Christians underestimate what Jesus' power can do in and through them. Christians have, again, dumbed down faith to acknowledging a list of doctrine. They do not expect genuine life change. They do not expect transformation. They do not think about being made into new creations in Christ. They do not believe that the Holy Spirit within them can truly guide and direct. They do not believe that they have the ear of the most powerful Being in the universe, ready to move on their behalf.

The Bible indicates that God intends Christians to be living billboards to the power of Christ to transform sinful humanity into the image of God.[46] If true, the result should not be a tepid trickle of marginal change, but a salvation that can produce a tree with an overwhelmingly good fruit. They need to begin to believe in a mighty God.

Second, concerning the bad bearing bad fruit, I think we overestimate the importance of being nice or accomplished. It seems harsh for Jesus to say that someone is only bearing bad fruit. Many non-Christians are nice people. Many have degrees or other accomplishments. How can Jesus say that they bear no good fruit?

It is essential to start by going back to the definition given earlier about what fruit is. Fruit is not being nice or accomplished. It is followers of Christ becoming like Jesus themselves and pointing people toward Him. This is important: it is not just pleasant or impressive things – it is becoming like Jesus and pointing people toward Him.

When you understand that, things become a little clearer. Even if a person is accomplishing much in his life, if they are not making him like Christ or pointing people to Christ, he is not bearing good fruit as defined by Christ. Even if a person is generally nice to be around, if he is not pointing people to Christ, he is not bearing good fruit.

Good fruit is not a "good life" the way that Americans usually define "the good life": a decent marriage, a couple kids, a nice house, and money to travel. You know, the American Dream. The Bible points followers of Christ toward the Kingdom of God, which has values that are antithetical to the American Dream.

I confess that I think both these explanations are helpful but incomplete. Still, Christians must face them squarely, whatever interpretation they use for these verses, knowing that they clearly point to fruit that is not hidden, but is obvious.

One final note on this "good tree" idea: the verses that follow the "good tree" passage directly address the "saying-you-believe-is-enough" teachers. Jesus continued in the Sermon on the Mount with these words:

> "*Not everyone who says to Me, 'Lord, Lord,*' will enter the kingdom of heaven, but he who *does the will* of My Father who is in heaven will enter."[47]

Jesus put a quick end to those Christians who would like to argue that empty "belief" is the dividing line between the followers of Christ and the outsiders. Here Jesus was immediately and abundantly clear: the true follower of Christ is the one who "does the will" of His Father. That is the dividing line. (I will explain in a minute the close connection between "doing the will of My Father" and fruitfulness.)

This teaching was immediately emphasized by the closing story in the Sermon on the Mount. It is about building your life "on the rock." It begins:

> "Therefore everyone who hears these words of [Mine] and *puts them into practice* is like a wise man who built his house on the rock. The rain came down, the streams rose, and the winds blew and beat against that house; yet it did not fall, because it had its foundation on the rock."[48]

The distinguishing characteristic is that the person puts the teaching of Jesus *into practice*. Again not an empty "belief" but obedience – an actual following of Christ and His teaching.

This truth figures prominently in how followers of Christ bear fruit, but first let me address the degree of fruitfulness Jesus envisioned.

How Much Fruitfulness Does Christ Expect?

Do you remember the iconic tree from the old Charlie Brown Christmas special? It was so small and spindly that even one ornament caused it to droop to the side. I know a man-made ornament is not the same thing as an apple growing on a fruit tree, but that pathetic little Charlie Brown tree is not a bad picture of the way many Christians think of potential spiritual fruitfulness. If you have any (and, again, they have come to view it as optional rather than a defining characteristic), it may just be one lone apple. After all, you are just a sinner saved by grace, so God cannot expect much from you. But, hey, at least you have something.

In contrast, Jesus shares a story in all three Synoptic gospels that paints a much different picture.[49] It is called the parable of the four soils. Here is what Jesus said:

> "A farmer went out to sow his seed. As he was scattering the seed, some

> fell along the path, and the birds came and ate it up. Some fell on rocky places, where it did not have much soil. It sprang up quickly, because the soil was shallow. But when the sun came up, the plants were scorched, and they withered because they had no root. Other seed fell among thorns, which grew up and choked the plants. Still other seed fell on good soil, where it produced a crop."[50]

He went on to explain the symbolism. The first type of soil (on the path and the birds ate it) represented

> "When anyone hears the message about the kingdom and does not understand it, the evil one comes and snatches away what was sown in his heart."[51]

The second type of soil represented people where "trouble or persecution" caused them to fall away.[52]

The third type of soil represented people where "the worries of this life and the deceitfulness of wealth choke" the seed, which rendered it "unfruitful."[53]

For reasons that I will confine to the endnotes, all three of these "soils" represented non-believers,[54] but the final soil was a picture of the follower of Christ.

Above, I only quoted part of what Jesus said about that fourth soil. Here is all of it:

> "Still other seed fell on good soil, where it produced a crop – a hundred, sixty, or thirty times what was sown."[55]

This is a picture of a life that does not merely produce a "Charlie Brown tree" harvest – this is a picture of an *abundant* harvest. This is an echo of the idea Jesus taught in John 15 when He said that His normal follower would "bear *much* fruit."[56] In this four soils parable is again the idea that a Christian is someone who does more than just feign empty "belief":

> "these are the ones who have heard the word in an honest and good heart, and hold it fast, and bear fruit with perseverance."[57]

Now, just how impressive is a harvest that is a hundred, sixty, or thirty times what was sown? One leading evangelical notes the average "planted seed to harvest seed" ratio in Palestine in that era was eight times what was sown.[58] Jesus promised thirty times, sixty times, even a hundred times. That means that Jesus spoke about fruitfulness that ranged from impressive to overwhelming.

People having different gifts, capacities, and circumstances leads to some bearing more than others, but even the smallest harvest that Jesus anticipated is nearly *four times* the normal harvest. In sum, Jesus expected an overflowing fruitfulness from His followers.

How Does Someone Bear More Fruit?

I have, I believe, already solidly proven my point: Christians have defined Christianity as a fruitless "belief" – mere mental assent to a list of theological dictates. Jesus expected people to obey His teaching and promised that doing so would result in obvious, overflowing fruitfulness. Christians are severely off course.

Certainly some will consider my Biblical analysis in this chapter to be inadequate and be untroubled by my arguments; others, though, may find these words convicting and desire to find a better way than what they have been given by most Christian leaders. Out of regard for the latter group, I will share Jesus' instructions on how to bear more fruit.

John 15 is the crucial chapter. In the analogy Jesus used, He was the "true vine" and His heavenly Father was the "vinedresser."[59] The followers of Jesus, in turn, were the "branches" coming off the "true vine." These branches were to bear fruit.[60]

Jesus was clear in John 15 that He intended for His followers to be fruitful. At least four times in ten verses He made this point:

> "every branch that *bears fruit*, [the Father] prunes it so that it may *bear more fruit*."[61]

> "As the branch cannot *bear fruit* of itself unless it abides in the vine, so neither can you unless you abide in Me."[62]

> "I am the vine; you are the branches; he who abides in Me and I in him, he *bears much fruit*."[63]

> "My Father is glorified in this, that you *bear much fruit*, and so prove to be My disciples."[64]

(Going back to a point made throughout this chapter, notice that in this last verse Jesus said that bearing much fruit was proof that a person was one of His disciples.) The point here is simple: God wants followers of Christ to be fruitful, and not just with a modest impact, but bearing "much fruit."

That raises an obvious question: how does a follower of Christ bear fruit? Fortunately, the passage answers that question. Followers of Christ bear fruit by abiding in Christ. Verses 4 and 5 are crucial. Jesus said:

> "*Abide in Me*, and I in you. As the branch cannot bear fruit of itself unless it abides in the vine, so neither can you *unless you abide in Me*. I am the vine, you are the branches; *he who abides in Me* and I in him, he *bears much fruit*, for apart from Me you can do nothing."[65]

So, then, bearing fruit happens when someone is "abiding" in Christ. What exactly does "abiding" mean? It simply means being close to someone or something. Tying into the vine analogy that Jesus used: when the vine and the branch are closely connected as they should be, there should be an uninterrupted flow from the vine that produces fruit in the branch.

That raises another obvious question: how does a follower of Christ abide in Him? Fortunately, the passage answers that question as well. Followers of Christ abide by keeping Jesus' commandments. Verse 10 is crucial:

> *"If you keep My commandments, you will abide* in My love; just as I have kept My Father's commandments and abide in His love."[66]

This makes sense when you think about it. If you are a follower of Jesus and therefore doing the specific things that Jesus commanded, you are naturally going to become more like Him and get closer to Him. This, again, stands in stark contrast to Christians' current teaching that a person can be a "believer" in Jesus without actively being someone who obeys what Jesus taught.

Allow me to share a mnemonic device that has helped me to remember this truth:

Obey ---> Abide ---> Abound

"Obey" leads to "abide" which leads to "abound." When a follower of Christ *obeys* the teachings of Jesus, it will lead to him *abiding* in Him (John 15:10). When a follower of Christ is *abiding* in Jesus, it will lead to him *abounding* in fruitfulness (John 15:4-5). "Abound" is just a way to say "bear much fruit" that is easier to remember with this mnemonic.

This is not the vision Jesus had for super-Christians; this is to be the normative Christian life. A follower of Christ will, by definition of being a follower of Christ, obey His teaching; this in turn will lead to his being close to Jesus (abiding in Him); this closeness will lead to a life of overflowing fruitfulness (abounding).

It is probably worth mentioning here that this path outlined by Christ is not the one that most preachers share when encouraging their congregations to grow spiritually or to have a great impact. If I were to summarize the standard Christian teaching in two words, it would be these: "try harder." You are not praying enough, you are not giving enough, you are not reading the Bible enough, you are not witnessing enough, you are not coming to church enough. You need to try harder.

Notice that Jesus' teaching in John 15 points us to two radically different words. If I were to summarize all of Jesus' teaching in John 15 on living a life of abundant fruitfulness, it would be these: "get closer." The fruitful life that Jesus desired to be normative for Christians is not found in our own redoubled efforts. After all, "apart from Me you can do nothing" Jesus said in verse 5.[67] No, Jesus pointed His followers toward being as close as possible to Him and then allowing the fruitfulness to naturally flow from that connection.

I will confine my thoughts on the best three places to start in this endeavor to the endnotes.[68] The fundamental point here is that the Bible teaches that as Christians get close to Christ abundant fruit will naturally flow. Therefore, if there is a lack of abundant fruit in Christians' lives, that is definitive evidence that they are not close to Christ.

To summarize, Jesus condemned the Pharisees for a lack of godly fruit. Christians are also lacking in godly fruit. The Pharisees focused their attention on obeying many rules. Christians do that, but have also redefined "belief" as an empty verbal assent while failing to teach the full picture of abundant life in Christ. For these reasons, Christians are failing to bear godly fruit.

Jesus cast a vision of fruitfulness that was necessary, obvious, and abundant. In John 15, He laid out in simple terms the path to that fruitfulness. Christians must face that their lack of fruitfulness is evidence they are more like the Pharisees than they are like Jesus.

Chapter Five

"He Who Is Forgiven Little, Loves Little"

Respectability, "good people," and Plan B

Many years ago, I was only partially through the sermon during an evening service when someone began to walk up the aisle. If you know much about conservative Christian churches, you know that "walking the aisle" to come to the altar is something that is encouraged, but it is supposed to happen at the close of worship, when the pastor gives the invitation. On that evening, this person was coming up the aisle at the "wrong time." (Nothing wrong with that – it was just unexpected.)

It was the "town drunk" who was walking forward. I stopped the sermon and sat down with him on the front pew. We talked and prayed, then he returned to the back pew and I restarted the sermon. Anytime someone comes forward it is a welcome sight, but what made this moment particularly meaningful is that the sermon I had been preaching was on God's concern for the poor. After the sermon was over, I thought, "What a Holy Spirit moment – I could not have illustrated that sermon any better than to have someone in such a struggling situation come forward to 'interrupt' the sermon."

The next morning, I received a call from someone who had been in the worship service. I smiled, anticipating her sharing how meaningful it had been. Instead, she began to ask about the church having a security plan in case "someone like that" showed up in future services. It broke my heart that she was so spiritually numb that she had completely missed what God had done.

Conservative Christian churches are filled with respectable people. That is not to say that respectable people are not also in need of God, but it is a telling statement when you consider that Jesus was generally surrounded with people from the margins of society. The Pharisees were among the respectable people in Jewish society at that time. In many churches, there is palpable discomfort when someone starts attending who is "not like us" (that is, not one of the respectable people). Don't believe me? Walk into the average church with a scraggly beard, Harley t-shirt, and two armfuls of tattoos and see if you get more hugs or sidelong glances.

This chapter is about forgiveness, grace, and respectability. Forgiveness and grace are words that Christians use a lot, but their respectability reveals that they do not understand those ideas as well as they think they do.

Simon the Pharisee and an Unwelcome Guest

Simon the Pharisee invited Jesus to his house for a meal.[1] The meal was interrupted, though, by an unexpected guest:

> When a woman who had lived a sinful life in that town learned that Jesus was eating at the Pharisee's house, she brought an alabaster jar of perfume, and as she stood behind [His] feet weeping, she began to wet [His] feet with her tears. Then she wiped them with her hair, kissed them and poured perfume on them.[2]

This is, to my thought, a beautiful sight, like my sermon interrupter. Simon, though, was shocked and dumbfounded. At the sight of this woman "anointing the feet of Jesus," he thought:

> "If this man were a prophet He would know who and what sort of person this woman is who is touching Him, that she is a sinner."[3]

Simon could not make sense of the fact that Jesus allowed this sinful woman to touch Him. As stated earlier, the Pharisees held the idea of "holiness by separation," so Simon here believed that if Jesus were actually holy He would separate Himself from people like this woman. Instead, Jesus seemed to welcome the woman's actions.

In response to Simon's thoughts (which the story presumes that Jesus knew), Jesus told him a story:

> "Two men owed money to a certain moneylender. One owed him five hundred denarii, and the other fifty. Neither of them had the money to pay him back, so he canceled the debts of both."[4]

A denarius was a denomination of money in that day, worth about a day's wage.

Having told His story, Jesus then posed a question to Simon: "Now which of them will love him more?"[5] Simon made the obvious choice: "I suppose the one who had the bigger debt canceled."[6] Jesus told Simon that he got the answer right and then lowered the boom:

> "Do you see this woman? I entered your house; you gave Me no water for My feet, but she has wet My feet with her tears and wiped them with her hair. You gave Me no kiss; but she, since the time I came in, has not ceased to kiss My feet. You did not anoint My head with oil, but she has anointed My feet with perfume. For this reason I say to you, her sins, which are many, have been forgiven, for she loved much; but he who is forgiven little, loves little."[7]

Jesus praised this woman's shameless expression of love toward Him. Those actions did not happen – this is important – in spite of the fact that she had sinned much, but *because* she had sinned much.

How did that happen? It looks something like this. The woman knew she had sinned greatly and was distant from God. In Jesus' person and in His message, she heard actions and words of *grace and forgiveness*. She eagerly pursued that possibility, with her desperate hope blinding her to what those in the room (like Simon the Pharisee) thought of her and her actions. She was so bold precisely because she was so hungry for grace and forgiveness. The typical Pharisee religious calculations left her with no hope of getting anywhere close to God; in Jesus, though, a door unexpectedly opened. She gratefully and joyfully walked through.

Thus, we come to Jesus' final statement in the above verses. Jesus offered grace and forgiveness to someone who was distant from God. Because of that, she loved Jesus much. That love led to Jesus' eagerness to forgive. It is precisely *because* she started so far from God that she loved Jesus and His forgiveness so much. She loved much because she had been forgiven of much. Just as important, though, is the final statement. The one who had been forgiven of little, loved little. It is here we find Pharisees and Christians living in all their glorious respectability.

Plan A and Plan B

This story is a dynamic example of the spiritual rearranging that Jesus did. Most Christians tout *grace and forgiveness* as superlative spiritual ideas, but they remain unaware of just how radical those concepts are. To understand the difference more clearly, consider what I will call Plan A and Plan B of interacting with God. In each case, I will pose four questions: what does God want most from us?; who is at an advantage?; why are they at an advantage?; and how should I respond?

Plan A is the standard morality approach utilized by the Pharisees as well as by most Christians today. I will briefly review it before more extensively unpacking Plan B as I compare the two.

Question #1 is "What does God want most from us?" The answer under Plan A is "be good." The Pharisees put great focus on trying to please God by following the myriad rules of the Mosaic Law. They were trying to be good people, according to the rules.

Question #2 asks "Who is at an advantage?" If the goal is to "be good," then who is the most likely to do that? The answer under Plan A is "the best of rule-keepers." The Pharisees were masters at this, going so far as to create hundreds of additional rules to the Law that God had originally given in an effort to better please Him.

Question #3 then follows, "Why are they at an advantage?" The answer under Plan A is that "they are not like those flagrant sinners." The Pharisees had great disdain for all the Jews who failed to be as passionate as they were in trying to keep the Law. It helped the Pharisees to know with confidence that they were God's favorites, because He obviously was appalled by the population at large and their spiritual apathy.

Question #4 concludes by asking, "How should I respond?" That answer under Plan A is "sin management." All people are fallen and therefore struggle with sin, but the Pharisees were experts at keeping those struggles under wraps. "Sin management" means that a person manages the public relations of his sins, keeping them hidden. It means that a person makes sure that whatever sins he commits do not become a public embarrassment. Being truly holy before God is left behind as one settles for the appearance of not having substantial sin problems in order to maintain respectability.

Plan B represents the approach Jesus is taking here in this story of Simon and the woman. It is an approach filled with *grace and forgiveness*. It is wildly different from Plan A. Here is a side-by-side comparison:

	Plan A	Plan B
What does God want most from us?	Be good	Love
Who is at an advantage?	Best of rule-keepers	Worst of sinners
Why are they at an advantage?	Not like those flagrant sinners	More forgiveness = more love
How should I respond?	Sin management	Confess who you really are

Question #1 is "What does God want most from us?" Plan B says that the answer is "love." When Jesus was asked what the greatest commandment was, He pointed people to two commandments both of which were focused on love (love God, love others).[8] In fact, He went so far as to say that the whole Law hung on those two things.

It is an astounding thought to consider: God wants *our* love. In the Luke 7 story, compare the woman's outward, shameless expression of unembarrassed love for Jesus to Simon's cool, intellectual, doctrinaire, prideful receiving of Christ. When you consider how many churches are filled with "respectable people," that is probably not a good sign. Why do churches so plainly and consistently fail to attract the brokenhearted and downtrodden? It points to Christians being Plan A people, like the Pharisees.

An honest analysis of the vast majority of churches would conclude that love is not the main defining characteristic of those congregations or the Christians who populate them. There are many believers who claim Christ, but not nearly as many who have tangible evidence in their lives that they love Him. There are few who are obvious and frequent in their expressions of love for Him. It is beside the point whether that love is expressed in an extroverted, bold manner like the Luke 7 woman or in a quiet, introverted way like a more reserved Christian might – whatever the form it takes, is my love for God the guiding characteristic of my religious faith?

What God ultimately wants from people is not merely checking a box for the right doctrine, but for them to live in His abundant love. Love is not a theoretical idea; it does not spring from doctrine. Love rises from the personal experience of having been helped, forgiven, saved, healed, and repaired. My maternal grandmother was a Depression Democrat. Once, as a joke, I asked her if she would vote for me if I ran for president as a Republican. Her response was an instant and emphatic "no." That did not arise from a dispassionate consideration of the alternatives for political allegiance. It arose from seeing her family and other families around her struggling to put food on the table and having FDR come through for them with jobs' programs. Whether it was those programs or World War II that ultimately ended the Great Depression was immaterial to her. What mattered was something to eat and seeing this political leader do something about it. There are loyalties and allegiances that are deeper than mere intellectual considerations.

God is after our love. Think of how much time is spent in children's Sunday School classes in churches teaching kids to "be good little boys and girls." It misses the larger context of the point of this whole thing: God wants us to love Him.

I know that many Christians reading this are thinking, "Are you just excusing sin? Are you saying it does not matter how we act?" I am not saying that. How we live our lives matters greatly. However, pursuing that obedience from the "be good" approach that Plan A offers is a recipe for failure. Obedience arising from a Plan B approach, however, has a strong chance of success, for reasons we will discuss momentarily.

Question #2 asks "Who is at an advantage?" Here the Plan B answer shocks: "the worst of sinners." What? How can this be? This is where we need to understand the radical nature of *grace and forgiveness*. The Pharisees' (and most Christians') approach pursues trying to be good by following the rules. The idea of grace posits the unavoidable failure of that approach.

Grace argues that our human attempts at obeying the rules to please God will fail because we cannot perfectly keep them. This will inevitably leave us short of God's standard. Grace puts forward that a person cannot earn her way to God. She must be saved *by grace*. That is, it must come as a free gift from God. Christians believe this happens through Christ's death and resurrection. When a person becomes a Christian, she receives it *by grace through faith*.[9] That is, her *faith* in Christ allows God to save her *by grace*. It is a gift. A person simply needs to recognize her spiritual need, humble herself before God, and ask for God's help. Obviously, this stands in stark contrast to attempts to get to God by being "the best of rule-keepers," trying to earn her way there.

Who is most likely to embrace this grace? It is those who are "the worst of sinners." It is those who understand how badly they have messed up and have no illusions of being "better than those people." Those in such a situation hear of the possibility of grace and leap at it. They know what an incredible offer is being made - and unlike those who are "the best of rule-keepers," their obvious sin (remember that they are not good at sin management) forces them to acknowledge they cannot earn their way to God. Remember that the question we are answering is not "Who needs grace?" – the obvious answer there is *everyone*. The question is "Who is at an advantage?"

and the nature of grace makes those who have great sin more likely to pursue it.

One way to put it is that grace "reverses the line." Think of an imaginary lineup of all the people arranged from the "good people" at the front to the "bad people" at the back. In Plan A thinking, those at the front of the line – the "good people" – are at an advantage in getting to God. They are, after all, at the front of the line morally (or, at least, the appearance of morality). Grace, though, "reverses the line." Imagine everyone in that line turning around and suddenly those who were at the end of the line find themselves at the front of the line. Through grace, those who started "at the end of the line" now find themselves the most likely to grasp onto God's invitation. We see this played out in Jesus' day as the "tax collectors and sinners" were found hanging out with Jesus.[10] This was not an idle phrase. It was the "worst" who flocked to Jesus and loved Him the most. Why? Because He embodied grace and that put them at the front of the line.

Many of you are thinking, "That is insane! You can't put the worst of sinners at the front of the line. That does not make any sense! It puts everything backwards. It is the 'good people' who God loves the most." If you feel that way, it is probably a sign that you now understand grace correctly for the first time. In his masterful explanation of salvation, Paul was forced to respond to that very issue. He wrote at the beginning of Romans 6:

> What shall we say then? Are we to continue in sin so that grace may increase? May it never be! How shall we who died to sin still live in it?[11]

Some trashed his argument for grace by saying, "Well, if that is the way that God saves people, then should not we just go out and sin all that we can?" Paul said, "May it never be!" Grace is not an excuse to keep on piling up sin; grace is the only means for gaining freedom from our sin.

Yes, it is scandalous. Yes, it is breathtaking. Yes, it is unfair. Why do you think the Pharisees were so furious at Jesus? He was trampling on their very approach to God. They thought they were at the front of the line and suddenly Jesus reversed the line.

Jesus told the respectable religious people of His day:

> "Truly I say to you that the tax collectors and prostitutes will get into the kingdom of God before you."[12]

He goes on to explain that the reason for this is that the respectable people "did not repent."[13] (Read: refused to publicly admit they were sinners.) This was why Jesus was accused of being "a friend of tax collectors and sinners."[14]

Paul got to this spiritual reality in his first letter to Timothy when he wrote:

> It is a trustworthy statement, deserving full acceptance, the Christ Jesus came into the world to save sinners, among whom I am foremost of all.[15]

If he was such a horrible sinner, why would Christ save him? Paul explained:

> Yet for this reason I found mercy, so that in me as the foremost, Jesus Christ might demonstrate his perfect patience as an example for those who would believe in Him for eternal life.[16]

Notice that Paul argues Christ saved him not *in spite of* the fact that he was a horrible sinner, but *because of* the fact that he was a horrible sinner.

The point of this is not to think, "Hey, I'm going to go sin as much as I can so that I'll be at the front of the line!" This is not about gaming the system, as if that were possible. Rather, when a person realizes that he needs God in his life, the one at an advantage is the person most likely to grab onto grace through faith. The surprising reality is that advantaged group is comprised of those who are unable to excuse their sin or talk themselves into believing that they really aren't that bad after all. In other words, the worst of sinners.

Question #3 then follows: "Why are they at an advantage?" The answer is that "more forgiveness = more love." It is a principle explicitly stated at the end of our Luke 7 story:

> "For this reason I say to you, her sins,
> which were many, have been forgiven,
> for she loved much; but he who is
> forgiven little, loves little."[17]

There is a symbiotic relationship between forgiveness and love. The more forgiveness you receive, the more love you are going to show. Simon did not even share the basic courtesies with Jesus when He came to the house; the massively forgiven woman outdid him in acts of extraordinary welcome and affection. Compare that to Christians who invite Jesus into their hearts, but then do little to make Him feel welcome. They call themselves Christians, yet are barely cordial to Christ in the claims He makes on their lives.

Another way to put it is this: there is a predictor of how much we will love God. Certainly other factors are in play, but the biggest factor is how much we have been forgiven. The woman *loved Jesus* more than Simon did. Period. And *love* is what God desires.

I do not think that most Christians appreciate just how big a game changer grace is – how much it alters everything, how much it turns religion on its head, how much it rearranges the natural order of things. Christians seem to mention grace only as the means by which someone is saved. It is more, though, than simply the name of the mechanism by which salvation happens. The very fact that it is the means by which someone is saved has an enormous influence on who gets saved, on who is most likely to be saved, and on who is at the front of the line. Grace is not earning salvation via good works or a good reputation, but is the acknowledgement that you can never in your own power be good enough. This means that those who were the least likely to be able to "earn their salvation" will be the most likely to jump at this new system.

Why would God do things this way? First, it is necessary because no one is sufficiently good to be able to earn her salvation.

Second, God has made it clear in the Bible that His preference is for the humble over the proud.[18]

The reality of grace is not being preached in most churches. The indisputable proof is in the respectability of those congregations. They are drawn from the front of the Plan A line. Certainly those people also need salvation, but if grace was understood and preached by Christians, their congregations would be filled with the same people Jesus attracted: the obviously sinful, the messed up, the ragged, the disenfranchised, those living in the margins, those with nowhere else to turn. Grace churches would be Plan B churches.

But they aren't. Dear Lord, that last sentence breaks my heart.

American churches are famous for what they are against. They are populated with the "good people" of the town. A few of the churches are good at loving each other (though most settle for merely being nice to each other), but that love is rarely directed toward those outside the church family, especially if they do not "look like us."

Christians have given lip service to the necessity of grace, but then continued to actually live out the Plan A "good person" approach. Adopting the Plan B approach I have detailed would literally frighten many congregants. Church would no longer be a safe and comfortable place; it would be a place of wild and unpredictable forgiveness that reaches to the very edges of society. Who knows who might walk through the door?

Question #4 continues by asking "How should I respond?" The Plan B answer is "confess who you really are." Attempts at "sin management" – looking good in public while hiding your worst sins – will not fool God. It can lead to lots of nice things being said at your funeral, but it will not help you at the Final Judgment.

In the Luke 7 parable, both of the debtors owed massive amounts of money. Sure, the second guy can take some solace that he does not owe as much as the first guy, but that does not put him one nickel closer to being able to actually pay his heaping debt. The quickness to look to the "not-as-bad-as" defense has long been a human tendency. "I am not perfect, but I am not as bad as him." From a Biblical perspective, though, a more analogous defense would be "Sure, I have killed someone, but at least I am not a serial killer like him." How well would that defense work before a jury? Not too well. You are guilty and deserving of death.

To use a different analogy, it is like jumping off the edge of the Grand Canyon. One person might just take a small step, while the other person might come running up and fling himself out as far as possible. Whether you take a small step or a flying leap, you are still going to end up dead at the bottom.

When it comes to "sin management," it is not that we do not have sin, because we do. It is that we as a culture have come to minimize it or deny it altogether. The tragic irony is that we think by denying and minimizing our sinfulness, we will get closer to God. In fact, it is by admitting our horrid sinfulness that we actually have greater opportunity to love God.

It is not that you need to go out and commit lots of horrible sins. (Again, Romans 6.) But you do need to acknowledge who you actually are and confess that reality – you are sufficiently bad to drive you into the arms of Christ. However, this requires you to admit that you are not a good person. All of us need the grace and forgiveness of Jesus. If I am a respectable person, one of the greatest impediments to me receiving God's grace and forgiveness is my desire to maintain my reputation as a respectable person. It is in many ways harder for me to grab onto that grace and forgiveness because I also want to hold onto my respectability. For those of us who look respectable, it is essential that we freely confess: "I am not a good person – I am a wretched sinner in need of God's grace." The fact that I am a respectable person makes it more difficult for me to say that than people like the woman at Simon's house, but I need to say it anyway. Throw away the sin management and grab eagerly onto the grace of Jesus.

I cannot adequately explain how much resistance I have gotten to this in my preaching. When I have preached that none of us are "good people," there is push back. Surely I do not mean that. Yes, I do – none of us are good people. Such preaching is not well received. Christians will even hold "good people" beliefs about non-Christians. I have heard countless times a believer talk about an unsaved friend or neighbor: "He is a good person; he just needs to get saved." What? If he is a good person, why does he need to be saved? By "good person," the believer actually means "he is nice to me," which is not the definition of being a good person.

A key to Plan B thinking is the simple but difficult personal acknowledgement: "I am a terrible sinner." No comparisons: "I have done a few bad things, but not as many as him." No excuses: "I have made mistakes, but there were extenuating circumstances." No shifting of blame: "I can be a pain, but you do not understand the home I was raised in." No qualifications: "That is a sin, but the rest of these might not be."

Conservative Christians are weak on repentance, as I will show in greater detail in the next chapter. They do not sufficiently explain to those thinking of becoming Christians that they must acknowledge that they are sinners and repent of those sins. In its place is a generic statement that "we are all sinners." That is true, but to become a Christian you need to face the fact that your individual sins were and are sufficiently numerous and heinous to require the death of the Son of God on a cross to even make your salvation possible. There is a substantial difference between the breezy "we are all sinners" and the pointed and painful recognition that I am a serious sinner who desperately needs divine forgiveness.

Our churches are filled with congregants who see themselves as "good people," not serious sinners. They need to embrace something I have often said: "I do not go to church because I am a good person; I go to church because I know I am not."

Christians are ardent supporters of Plan A. It is obvious from how different their congregations are from the crowds that surrounded Jesus. It is obvious in the lack of passionate love for Christ. It is obvious in how much more they resemble the somber Simon than the shameless woman.

Christians love little because they believe they have been forgiven of little. That is not an accurate assessment of their need for forgiveness, but represents how much forgiveness they think they need. The evidence indicates they do not understand the radical grace that Plan B represents. It is a tragic irony that for a people who cite *grace and forgiveness* so often, they actually understand them so little. Christians instead are, as a group, respectable people skilled at sin management. In all this, they show themselves to have missed the heart of Jesus' gospel path for getting to God. *Grace and forgiveness* lead to thankful love, which is exactly what God desires. Christians, though, are too busy trying to appear good to have time to love God.

Chapter Six

"You Are Israel's Teacher and Do You Not Understand These Things?"

Nicodemus, the basics, and Paul's theological masterpiece

A friend of mine always laughed when he told me this story. One evening, he was at a high school basketball game seated near a local preacher. He had long felt that the preacher was a little too full of himself and his Bible knowledge.

That night, in the course of conversation, a controversial Scriptural subject came up. The preacher confidently asserted his belief and then said, "That's from Jude chapter 2."

"Preacher," my friend replied, "Jude only has one chapter!"

There was a momentary pause before the preacher muttered, "Well, of course. I was just testing you."

That tale sits in the back of my mind as a reminder that just because someone is confident in his religious knowledge does not mean that confidence is justified.

Given their passion for the Law and their dedicated obedience to it, one would presume that the Pharisees were experts in all things religious. It comes as a shock, then, that early in John's gospel Jesus accused a leading Pharisee of abject spiritual ignorance. This happened in John 3, which culminates in the most famous verse in the Bible: John 3:16. It is what comes earlier in John 3, though, that is the focus for this chapter.

This is the story of a conversation between Jesus and a man named Nicodemus, who was "a man of the Pharisees . . . a member of the Jewish ruling council."[1] He was not just a "pew sitter" – this was someone who was a leading figure in Jewish religious life. Jesus intrigued him, but he came to Jesus "at night" because he was concerned about what his fellow Pharisees would think.[2] He acknowledged up front that they had been talking about Jesus:

> "Rabbi, we know that You have come from God as a teacher; for no one can do these signs that You do unless God is with him."[3]

Jesus was apparently not interested in a polite exchange of compliments because He responded with a stark spiritual statement:

> "I tell you the truth, no one can see the kingdom of God unless He is born again."[4]

This made no sense to Nicodemus, who incredulously replied:

> "How can a man be born when he is old? Surely he cannot enter a second time into his mother's womb to be born!"[5]

Nicodemus had no idea to what Jesus was referring. Jesus was talking about spiritual things, but Nicodemus was thinking literally. Jesus kept His foot on the gas:

> "I tell you the truth, no one can enter the kingdom of God unless he is born of water and the Spirit. Flesh gives birth to flesh, but the Spirit gives birth to spirit. You should not be surprised at [My] saying, 'You must be born again.' The wind blows wherever it pleases. You hear its sound, but you

> cannot tell where it comes from or where it is going. So it is with everyone born of the Spirit."[6]

Jesus made a stark distinction between matters of the "flesh" and matters of the "spirit." These ideas to Jesus' mind were apparently basic spiritual truths. Nicodemus, though, quizzically responded: "How can this be?"[7]

Jesus laid out truths that made little sense to Nicodemus. The Pharisee had no idea what to do with them. Jesus was unimpressed and said so:

> "You are Israel's teacher and do you not understand these things?"[8]

Ouch. Not much slack there. Jesus continued:

> "I tell you the truth, we speak of what we know, and we testify to what we have seen, but still you people do not accept our testimony. I have spoken to you of earthly things and you do not believe; how then will you believe if I speak of heavenly things? No one has ever gone into heaven except the one who came from heaven – the Son of Man. Just as Moses lifted up the snake in the desert, so the Son of Man must be lifted up, that everyone who believes in [Him] may have eternal life."[9]

Presumably the "we speak of what we know" referred to Jesus and those following Him while the "you people" referred to the Pharisees and those in their theological camp.[10] Jesus said that He was "from heaven" (He was the "Son of Man") and that Nicodemus did not even understand "earthly things." The reference to Moses and being "lifted up" points toward the cross on which Jesus would die. Jesus' words here could be summarized in three parts: you people do not believe what I am preaching ("do not accept our testimony"), you have not understood even elementary truths ("earthly things and you do not believe"), and you have no idea what the plan of God is ("the Son of Man must be lifted up").

Nicodemus was a leading religious authority of his day and yet Jesus found him to be almost completely lacking in spiritual insight. The ideas Jesus shared were not peripheral ones, but were at the heart of what God was doing in the world. Nicodemus was a religious expert whom Jesus found spiritually clueless. These were matters that Jesus believed Nicodemus should know ("You are Israel's teacher and do you not understand these things?"). In fact, He was appalled that he did not.

Experts in Religion, Beginners in Spirituality

One way to summarize Jesus' characterization of Nicodemus and the Pharisees here in John 3 is *experts in religion but beginners in spirituality*. There is no doubt that the Pharisees were the religious experts of their day. There is no doubt that they took their religion seriously. There is no doubt they were quick to enforce their religious rules and criticize those who dared break them, as Jesus frequently did. Jesus Himself acknowledged here that Nicodemus was "Israel's teacher," which was not to say that he had sufficient knowledge but that he was filling that role in society.[11]

Yet even though they were the self-appointed *experts in religion*, Jesus clearly regarded Nicodemus as a *beginner in spirituality*. For our purposes here, I am defining religion as the man-made rules and regulations of getting to God and spirituality as the wisdom of knowing how God really interacts with humanity and how to pursue more of that experience. Nicodemus could not make heads or tails of the spiritual truths that Jesus shared with him. "Born again"? "The wind blows wherever it pleases"? "How can this be?"

Think about what this means. Here we have a leading religious expert who was clueless about what Jesus presented as Spirituality 101. We might expect him to be slightly off center or missing the last ten percent of the needed insight, but to have him stand there unable to make sense of Jesus' opening words was an unexpected and embarrassing sight.

Is it possible that Christians are in a similar predicament as Nicodemus? Could it be that they are the self-appointed religious experts in American society and yet lack an awareness of how God actually works in the world? Are Christians *experts in religion but beginners in spirituality*? I believe a solid case can be made in this direction.

I will first examine the core salvation message that conservative Christians share and consider whether it lines up with the Bible's teaching and then more briefly examine two other central issues where Christians are surprisingly lacking. My goal is to prove that while Christians are widely considered experts in religion, they, in fact, are either ignorant of or dismissive of some of the most central spiritual truths.

The Four Parts of Paul's Theological Masterpiece

The first half of the book of Romans is widely considered by Biblical scholars to be Paul's theological masterpiece. I agree with them: the first eight chapters of Romans are the clearest explanation in the Bible of what this new salvation from Jesus actually looks like. Certainly the gospel passages about Jesus' death and resurrection are crucial to an understanding of how Christ made salvation possible, but Romans 1-8 gives an unparalleled explanation of how to receive this salvation and what it entails.

The standard Christian message on salvation is essentially this: *Jesus died on the cross for your sins and you can be saved by believing in the death and resurrection of Christ*. That is something that the Bible affirms, but it is *only part* of the salvation story. Specifically, in Paul's masterpiece, that is the second of four parts. The central point I intend to make is this: it is not that Christians are preaching a false gospel; the problem is that they are preaching a woefully incomplete gospel. And the consequences of this error are *directly responsible* for much of the shameful lack of fruitfulness in their churches.

Romans 1-8 can be divided up into four pieces.

First, there is the need for repentance. Most people thinking of repentance envision a long-haired guy standing on the corner with a sign that says, "The end is near!" The Bible's idea of repentance simply means an acknowledgement of sin and a 180-degree change of direction. Becoming a Christian starts with the recognition that you have been walking down the wrong path spiritually and need to change. You recognize you are a sinner, so you repent of your sin with the intent to start in another direction.

Paul starts Romans by detailing substantial wrongs that some people do. He draws the reader in as you think, "Yeah, what they are doing is terrible." Having drawn you in, Paul begins chapter 2 with this:

> Therefore you have no excuse, everyone of you who passes judgment, for in that which you judge another, you condemn yourself; for you who judge practice the same things.[12]

It is easy to condemn other people's sins, but Paul asserts that we need to recognize that we have a sin problem, too. Paul argues that all people are in the same boat when he writes in chapter 3:

> "There is no one righteous, not even one."[13]

A potential believer in Christ has to begin by admitting he is a sinner and in need of help. He needs to repent of his sin. The person cannot hold onto the belief that he is a "good person." After all, if you are a good person and can get to God on your own, then Jesus was a fool because He died for people who did not need saving.

Second, believe in Jesus' death and resurrection. As previously mentioned, this is the part that Christians focus on. Romans 5:8 reads:

> But God demonstrates His own love toward us, in that while we were yet sinners, Christ died for us.[14]

The Bible teaches that Jesus sacrificed Himself for humanity. Through His sacrifice, a door was opened for God to be able to forgive those who put their faith in Jesus.

Third, you are made a new creation in Christ. God does not just forgive the person who repents of his sin and believes in Jesus' death and resurrection – He also gives him a new heart:

> knowing this, that our old self was crucified with Him, in order that our body of sin might be done away with.[15]

Your old spiritual self is dead and a new spiritual being is alive. The idea here is that the new believer has been transformed into a new spiritual creation. As Paul wrote in one of his other epistles:

> Therefore, if anyone is in Christ, he is a *new creation*; the old is gone, the new has come![16]

Christians believe this to be the fulfillment of the Old Testament promise that God made:

> "I will give you a *new heart* and put a new spirit in you; I will remove from you your heart of stone and give you a heart of flesh. And I will put [My] Spirit in you."[17]

This creation of a new nature is crucial and almost completely overlooked by Christians, especially in gospel presentations. In saving people, God also transforms them spiritually into people who are capable of living for Him by making them into new creations. Christians frequently say, "I am only a sinner saved by grace," which would lead one to presume little chance of living a spiritually victorious life. That statement is not Biblically true, though. The Scriptural truth is that the Christian *was* a sinner saved by grace at the moment of salvation, but upon being saved is transformed by God into a new creation in Christ, fully capable of living victoriously. So, and this is a crucial distinction, a Christian should say that he *was* a sinner saved by grace but has *now* become a new creation in Christ.

This does not mean that a Christian will not sin. We still have the "fleshly" part of our nature with which to deal.[18] The key distinction is that after salvation the *core of who I am* is a new creation in Christ. This is my central identity. Yes, I still have to fight temptation, but I do so with *the nature of who I am having been changed*. As such, I am able to move forward anticipating victory and not resigned to inevitable spiritual defeat. God has changed who I am at the soul level.

Finally, you walk forward in the power of the Holy Spirit. Jesus emphasized, in the final few hours before His death, that He would send a "Helper" to His followers after He left this world.[19] That Helper, of course, is the Holy Spirit. Christians are given God's own presence to be with them.

Paul writes in Romans 8:14:

> For all who are being led by the Spirit
> of God, these are the sons of God.[20]

God intends to walk with Christians each step of the way to provide them with guidance, strength, and encouragement. A Christian is not left by God to make the needed changes to his life by his own abilities; rather, an intrinsic part of the divine plan is divine empowerment within each believer. Sadly, in the modern church the Holy Spirit is often only mentioned in the context of arguing over Pentecostal speaking in tongues.

The Holy Spirit is involved because God wants Christians to be able to actually live for Him, not just know about Him. God provides followers of Christ all the resources they need to be spiritually victorious and fruitful.

To summarize Paul in Romans 1-8:
1. Repent of your sins.
2. Believe in Jesus' death and resurrection.
3. You are made a new creation in Christ.
4. You walk forward in the power of the Holy Spirit.

Current Conservative Christian Gospel Presentations

Having laid out Paul's explanation of salvation in the greatest theological book of the Bible, let us consider whether contemporary gospel presentations reflect it. Below, I will name the organizations I am quoting not primarily out of a desire to censure them, but simply from the necessity of illustrating that these are mainstream practices.

Again, the assertion put forth here is this: Christians are preaching an incomplete gospel. They are, at best, only sharing one-and-a-half of the above four points, and usually simply one of those points. For a group who are so proud of their self-proclaimed faithfulness to the Bible, repeatedly committing such a substantial oversight on so significant an issue is stunning. The consequence of their failure is, figuratively and literally, damning.

Evangelical parachurch organization Campus Crusade for Christ (recently rebranded as "Cru") titles its gospel presentation "How to Know God Personally."[21] According to them, you can achieve that by pursuing four "principles":

Principle 1: God loves you and offers a wonderful plan for your life.

Toward proving this, they quote John 3:16 ("God so loved the world that He gave His one and only Son, that whoever believes in Him shall not perish, but have eternal life.") and John 10:10 on having "abundant life" in Christ.

It is probably worth noting that while the Bible does affirm that God loves people, the idea that He has a "wonderful plan" for each believer's life is something of a conservative Christian creation. It arises from Jeremiah 29:11:

> "For I know the plans I have for you," declares the Lord, "plans to prosper you and not to harm you, plans to give you hope and a future."[22]

If this verse is taken in isolation from the rest of Scripture, it certainly can be transformed into a "wonderful plan" prooftext. Taken in the larger Biblical context, though, we know that God does desire to bless His children, but that involves making their lives better, not necessarily easier. It includes challenging ideas like self-denial and self-sacrifice, carrying each other's burdens and carrying your cross.[23] This, of course, is nothing like what an unsaved person would take from "a wonderful plan for your life." They would likely visualize it as some embodiment of the American Dream. As presently used, the "wonderful plan" terminology is at best misleading; at worst, dishonest. I am not denying that God in His wisdom has insight into the path He desires for a believer to travel; it just looks nothing like what an unsaved person would take from "wonderful plan for your life." It is more the language of self-actualization than Biblical terminology.

Principle 2: All of us sin and our sin has separated us from God.

Romans 3:23 ("All have sinned and fall short of the glory of God") is quoted to prove that all humanity has sinned and Romans 6:23 ("The wages of sin is death") that we are separated from God.

Principle 3: Jesus Christ is God's only provision for our sin. Through Him we can know and experience God's love and plan for our life.

Romans 5:8 ("God demonstrates His own love toward us, in that while we were yet sinners, Christ died for us") as well as other passages (1 Corinthians 15:3-6 and John 14:6) are cited to prove this.

Principle 4: We must individually receive Jesus Christ as Savior and Lord; then we can know and experience God's love and plan for our lives.

Three passages are cited to prove this, including Ephesians 2:8-9 ("By grace you have been saved through faith; and that not of yourselves, it is the gift of God; not as a result of works, that no one should boast.").

That is a basic summary of the Campus Crusade for Christ "gospel presentation."

Did you notice what is missing?

The presentation is focused on point #2 of the four points from Romans 1-8: "believing in Jesus." While that is obviously important, they have neglected points 1, 3, and 4. While there is a mention of our sinfulness, there is never an actual call to repent of sins (Paul's first point). There is absolutely no explanation of becoming a new creation in Christ and having a new heart (Paul's third point). In fact, the only thing approximating it in the Cru presentation is a sub-point under their "Principle 4" that "When we receive Christ, we experience a new birth." Given the rest of the presentation, the most someone would presume is that "new birth" means they are being "born again," but there would be no thought of a change of spiritual character but rather merely spiritual position (i.e. that you "got saved").[24] Finally, there is no talk in the main Cru presentation about the presence of the Holy Spirit as a helper in the life of the follower of Christ. There is a passing reference to the Holy Spirit in a graphic later in the presentation, but no explanation of what that means.

In sum, the Campus Crusade for Christ presentation of what knowing God looks like is almost completely focused on *one-fourth of the actual Biblical plan.*

Perhaps this is an exception? Sadly, it is typical. Here is another example – notice the similarities. The gospel presentation that is shared on Billy Graham's site is entitled "Begin Your Journey To Peace."[25] Four steps are given:

Step 1: God loves you and has a plan for you!

As with the Cru presentation, John 3:16 and John 10:10 are quoted.

Step 2: Man is sinful and separated from God.

Again, Romans 3:23 and Romans 6:23 are quoted.

Step 3: God sent His Son to die for your sins!

Romans 5:8 is cited as the main proof, as with the previous example.

Step 4: Would you like to receive God's forgiveness?

Although no Scripture is given, the text under this point does at least say, "All you have to do is believe you are a sinner, that Christ died for your sins, and ask His forgiveness. Then turn from your sins – that's called repentance." While the order is different than Paul's (it puts asking for forgiveness inexplicably *after* the believing in Jesus), there is at least a mention of repentance. Certainly, it is very slight in comparison to the pointed and lengthy time that Paul gives to it in Romans, but under the circumstances we should perhaps give a half-credit for including any mention at all.

So Billy Graham, the greatest American Christian name of the last century, in his website's gospel presentation, gets one-and-a-half of Paul's four points. Even if you consider the repentance discussion to be sufficient, that only brings it up to *half* what Paul shared in his explanation of the gospel.

These two are both similar to the "Roman Road" that is a standard salvation presentation among Christians. In fact, it is probably not pressing the issue to call it *the* standard salvation presentation among Christians. What is the Roman Road?

1. **Romans 3:23.**

   All have sinned.

2. **Romans 6:23.**

   Everyone deserves spiritual death for their sins.

3. **Romans 5:8.**

Jesus died for humanity.

4. Romans 10:9.

Believe in Jesus and you will be saved.

Again, as with the previous two examples, we see an incomplete gospel presentation. Here again only one of the four points is shared.

Obviously, there will be Christians who will strongly object to these arguments. They will say, "The other parts are important, but you have to start by getting people to believe in Jesus! The other truths can be shared later."

The proper response involves two points. First, in the interest of people knowing what exactly it means to be a Christian, I believe that all four truths are essential enough to be included in the basic presentation. The omitted points are not extraneous material – they are fundamental to understanding what it means to be a Christian.

Second, for those who contend that what was shared in the Cru, Billy Graham, and Roman Road gospel presentations are sufficient, I have a question: what would be the outcome if you just told people that they need to "believe in Jesus" without sharing the reality of new creation or the necessity of following Christ? You would get a bunch of people who say they are Christians, but who bear no fruit and have no life change. That is *exactly what we have now in America*: many, many people who claim to be Christians but who bear no signs of spiritual fruitfulness in their lives whatsoever.

Christians' failure to preach the whole gospel has *directly led* to this situation. If fruitfulness is a sign of true salvation, then church leaders, by espousing incomplete doctrine, have led those people to a false assurance of salvation.

It is worth pausing to emphasize what a great and grave sin this discussion is laying at Christians' door: millions of people who honestly believe that they are spiritually right with God despite a complete lack of godly fruitfulness. They have this assurance simply because they said at some point in their life that they "believe in Jesus" and a pastor or church leader assured them that completed the spiritual process. They have that misplaced confidence because pastors and church leaders gave them that confidence by not sharing the whole gospel with them. This false confidence actually makes it much harder for them to genuinely become a follower of Christ because they are convinced that they are already right spiritually. This is spiritual blood on the hands of conservative Christian pastors and leaders.

Many will object that there are passages that say that all you have to do is believe and you will be saved. True enough. But it is essential that everyone involved understand what the term "believe" actually means. Is it a mere mental assent to a list of doctrines ("Yes, Jesus came in the flesh. Yes, Jesus died on the cross. Yes, Jesus rose from the dead.") or is it becoming a follower of Christ? For it to be the latter (which is the correct answer), are the third and fourth of Paul's points not crucially important? Does "believe" as it is used in the Bible not mean to trust and invest your whole life in this Person? Does that not include understanding what God has done in you spiritually as part of putting your faith in Jesus?[26] Is this breathtaking oversight not definitive proof that Christians are *experts in religion but beginners in spirituality*? They are well-versed in their standard evangelistic presentation, yet blissfully unaware of the degree to which it fails to embody the full gospel.

Two Additional Examples

The failure of Christians to preach a complete understanding of the Bible's vision of salvation is the most substantive way they are *experts in religion but beginners in spirituality*. There are numerous other issues, though, where their spiritual depth is less than impressive. I will limit myself to two.

1. Obedience.

Christ expects Christians to actually live out His teaching. This idea is largely lost among Christians, again under the auspices of incorrectly defined "belief." Christians push the idea that you simply need to "believe in Jesus" and you have accomplished the bulk of the necessary spiritual transaction. Any obedience beyond that is simply gravy – it is a nice addition, but not necessary. This is shown in the typical altar call in an conservative Christian church. As was alluded to in the previous section, such a call touts the necessity of coming forward to "believe in Jesus." Apparently nothing beyond this is expected. This hollowed-out definition of belief leads to the similarities in behavior between Christians and non-church-goers. The moral choices of those two groups are depressingly similar, indicating a lack of obedience of Christians to the life-altering teaching of Christ.

Is the necessity of obedience as a defining characteristic of being a Christian something that the Bible clearly indicates? Yes, as multiple passages attest:

> "Not everyone who says to Me, 'Lord, Lord,' will enter the kingdom of heaven, but *he who does the will of My Father* who is in heaven will enter."[27]
>
> "Therefore everyone who hears these words of [Mine] and *puts them into practice* is like a wise man who built his house on the rock."[28]
>
> "For whoever *does the will of My Father* who is in heaven, he is My brother and sister and mother."[29]
>
> "If *anyone chooses to do God's will*, he will find out whether [My] teaching comes from God or whether I speak on [My] own."[30]
>
> "He who *has My commandments and keeps them is the one who loves Me*; and he who loves Me will be loved by My Father, and I will love him and will disclose Myself to him."[31]

> "If anyone loves Me, *he will keep My word*."³²

> "*If you keep My commandments*, you will abide in My love."³³

All of these quotes come straight from the mouth of Jesus Himself. He made it abundantly clear that His expectation was obedience as a part of being a Christian. Indeed, how could you be a *follower* of Christ if you are unwilling to actually *follow* His teaching?

Despite this overwhelming evidence, Christians consistently fail to teach and preach the obligation of Christians to obey the teaching of Jesus. Instead, they have allowed their focus on being saved by grace through faith to blind them to what must be the result of that salvation. Here we have a fundamental matter that defines what being a Christian looks like and Christians have shown that they "do . . . not understand these things" (or, at least, have chosen to ignore these things). They have so much religious knowledge, yet are missing a point of basic spirituality as central as what walking as a Christian looks like. They are experts in their religion, but seriously lacking even concerning such a basic spiritual matter. How is it possible to know and teach so much of the Bible and yet consistently miss something this key? Is it definitive proof that Christians are *experts in religion but beginners in spirituality*?

2. Lose your life.

Here is one of Jesus' teachings that sounds counter-intuitive:

> "For whoever wishes to save his life will lose it; but whoever loses his life for My sake will find it."³⁴

This initially gives the appearance of some sort of Buddhist guru's mystery wisdom, but a careful consideration makes the point much more straightforward. Jesus here is giving a path toward a spiritually meaningful life. The human tendency is for a person to do what they want to do. In fact, American culture is particularly bad about this idea of self-fulfillment. "The whole point of life is to pursue your dreams." "Your life focus should be on discovering who you are." "You should do what makes you happy." This so permeates American popular culture as to be a cliché. More importantly, though, it is not only taken as a given but also as obviously and undeniably true.

Jesus disagreed. He did not counsel His followers to pursue self-fulfillment. He told His followers that they needed to put following His teaching ahead of their personal desires and goals. Certainly there will be times when the two coincide, but when they do not His instruction is to take precedence. This initially seems a painful sacrifice, but Jesus promised an impressive outcome. If the believer will "lose his life" by following Jesus' teaching, he will discover that he actually finds his life – that is, he will find a meaningful and fruitful life. Conversely, if he tries to "save his life" by clinging to his own desires and goals, it will turn out that he will actually lose his life – that is, he will find his life to be without ultimate purpose and value. According to Jesus, the door to a worthwhile life is not through self-fulfillment, but through self-denial. Though that sounds difficult, that is exactly what Jesus counseled earlier in this same passage:

> "If anyone wishes to come after Me,
> he must deny himself."[35]

This is not the easiest path, but it is the road of discipleship. Many will object that they will have to give up much that is valuable to them in order to pursue this. That is exactly what Jesus has in mind:

> "If anyone wishes to come after Me,
> he must deny himself, and take up his
> cross and follow Me."[36]

Here the idea of taking up your cross speaks of sacrifices in life far more often than a literal carrying of a cross. The path that Christ illuminated for His followers was a path of self-denial, sacrifice, and losing your life. These are deep spiritual waters, but they lie at the heart of what Jesus envisioned as the path of being His disciple.

What might this look like in someone's life? Take the hypothetical example of a young woman with the desire to become a doctor. The ideas of "losing your life" and "denying yourself" do not mean that she is barred from pursuing her goal, but that in that pursuit she is to put the guidance and instruction of Christ above her own desires. As she prays about that career choice, she feels a peace from God and so she moves forward into medicine. Later, as she considers the field in which she will specialize, it is her desire to pursue surgery. As she prays, though, she senses that she is being led by God toward family practice. Even though that is not her first choice, but she understands that she is to obey Christ even when it disrupts her plans. She understands that Christ has the right to guide her life and that in those situations where her will and God's will seem to disagree, she is to "lose her life" and obey God. (I experienced this in my life as I desired to pursue a law degree but sensed strongly God calling me to be a pastor. As a Christian, it was my duty to "deny myself" and obey God.) Around this same time, her boyfriend suggests that they move in together. Knowing how common that is these days, she is tempted to say yes, but she knows that the Bible's teaching on sexual purity means it is not God's will for her life. She again "denies herself," again trusting that God knows best.

As Christians make the difficult choices to "deny yourself," "carry your cross," or "lose your life," they do so believing that even in the challenges God is acting toward us out of love. He is not being punitive or petty. It may be that He knows this action will eventually be destructive to our lives. It may be that He needs us in a strategic position to bring about His larger mission. It may be it is part of growing us spiritually. Whatever the reason in our particular situation, we understand that these teachings are an intrinsic part of what the life of a follower of Christ looks like.

These ideas are embarrassingly absent from modern Christians discussion. Far too many Christian books are self-help books with a few Bible verses tossed in for flavoring (*Your Best Life Now*, anyone?). The "wisdom" of such books sounds like the self-fulfillment gospel preached by the rest of culture. So, too, are the sermons radiating from most Christian pulpits. Nothing radical or countercultural on these points – just generic self-fulfillment with a prayer at the end. Christians claim to be religious experts and yet they have almost completely abandoned even the thought of these fundamental spiritual principles. Even worse, they do not even seem to be aware that they are supposed to be preaching something different. Undoubtedly there are preachers who consider these truths too radical for their congregations and therefore make a conscious decision to avoid them. Most pastors, though, seem oblivious to the self-fulfillment waters in which they happily swim. Here again, we find that Christians are experts in religion (in this case, the gospel of self-fulfillment), but beginners at the spiritual truths of Christ. How is it possible to know and teach so much Bible and yet consistently miss something this key? Is it definitive proof that Christians are *experts in religion but beginners in spirituality*?

I will limit myself to those examples. I could continue with an exposition of Jesus' teaching on how humbling yourself will lead to God exalting you,[37] on the counterintuitive truths of the Beatitudes,[38] on the vanity of gaining all that the world considers important,[39] the financial freedom of the way of Christ,[40] or numerous other examples. The consistent point is that Christians claim to be the religious experts of the culture, yet are seriously lacking when it comes to the actual content of the gospel. World-renowned United Methodist pastor Will Willimon once mused that if his denomination was asked to posit the heart of their beliefs, they would likely offer: "Be nice."

Where is the wisdom that cuts against all that the world typically teaches? Where is the insight into the heart of God that leads to lives standing in stark contrast to business as usual? Where is the rejection of the shallowness of American culture's focus on money and fame to live for more meaningful things? Why do so many Christian sermons sound like a generic morality lesson rather than peeking into secret insight? Why do most Christian books mimic standard self-help patterns rather than opening eyes to a completely new approach to life? Christians are indisputably religious, but seem to be sorely lacking in spiritual insight.

Further, they have apparently allowed themselves to be satisfied with their standard theological answers. They spend much more time defending the religious ideas they find acceptable than they do humbly seeking greater spiritual depth. As a result, their churches are detailed in the religion they uphold and proclaim, but lacking in spiritual power. How lacking? Here is a question to ponder: if tomorrow the Holy Spirit ceased to show up to empower anything that happened in American churches, how long would it take most of those churches to notice that anything had changed? For an embarrassing number, church life would roll on unaffected, a testimony to the lack of actual dependence on Spiritual insight.

Christians are undoubtedly among the most religious people of their culture, but so were the Pharisees. Christians' failure to be Christlike, their generic morality preaching, their failure to teach the counterintuitive instruction of Jesus, and their lack of Spiritual power all point to a situation like Nicodemus'. Christians, like the Pharisees, are *experts in religion but beginners in spirituality*. If this accusation were true, American Christianity would have a lot of religion, but little transformation; lots of religious talk, but few genuinely Christlike people; many churches, but little mercy. Exactly as it is.

How can Christians claim to be the most passionate about God and the most devoted to His Word and yet live so blindly to all these essential spiritual concepts? How can they claim to have the answers to finding God while retaining so great a blind spot at the center of their belief? How is it possible to know and teach so much of the Bible and yet consistently miss concepts this key? Is it definitive proof that Christians are *experts in religion but beginners in spirituality*? Even when it comes to fundamental spiritual truths, would Jesus say to Christians:

> "You are teachers and do you not understand these things?"

Chapter Seven

"You Do Not Know the Scriptures"

Bible study, confidence, and Tiny Tim

We were all sitting in the choir loft behind the play scenery. The pulpit had been removed and a set had been constructed on the main platform, leaving the choir loft for the actors to sit out of sight. Our church did a drama every year and this year's play was a variation on Scrooge and Tiny Tim. We were enjoying a break in the practice.

I was a teen, recently saved, sitting there with a couple of the adult actors. One was Bob, our church's youth pastor, and the other was Roger, one of the leaders in our congregation. The talk turned to a theological point (the years have erased the specifics) and these two men started talking about what the Bible said about it. This was not an argument – they were fundamentally in agreement – but rather a discussion. They were quoting verses and explaining how various parts of the Bible came together on that subject.

I remember sitting there being *so* impressed. These guys *knew so much* about the Bible. In contrast, as a recent convert, I knew relatively little and was pretty clueless about a whole host of issues. (I remember Bob sharing a Sunday School lesson on euthanasia. I sat there wondering why he was teaching about children in China.[1]) In that choir loft, as a young believer I looked up to these guys as mature Christians *because they had so much Bible knowledge*.

It is initially surprising that the major opposition to Jesus was a people who were serious about their Bible study. One might expect that a group opposing Christ would hold the Law and the Prophets in as much contempt as they held Him. Instead, we are faced with a troubling fact that raises all sorts of perplexing thoughts: the enemies of God's Son were devoted to God's Word.

Proving the Pharisees' passion for the Bible is simple because it was deeply a part of who they were. They were so intense about obeying the Mosaic Law that they created many additional regulations to "help people" obey those original laws. Of course, as discussed elsewhere in this book, those additional regulations had the opposite of the intended effect, driving people away from God because they felt that following so many rules was a heavy burden impossible to fulfill. The Pharisees' frequent complaint was that Jesus had failed to do what was "lawful," further showing that their primary focus was on faithfulness to the rules.

The Pharisees considered themselves the experts on the Scripture. One colorful example of this is recorded in John 7 when the chief priests and the Pharisees sent the temple guards to arrest Jesus.[2] They returned empty-handed, much to their bosses' frustration:

> the chief priests and Pharisees . . . said to [the temple guards], "Why did you not bring Him?" The officers answered, "Never has a man spoken the way this man speaks."[3]

The Pharisees' response revealed how highly they thought of their own Scripture knowledge:

> "You have not also been led astray, have you? No one of the rulers or Pharisees has believed in Him, has he? But this crowd which does not know the Law is accursed."[4]

They clearly saw themselves as the final authority in Scripture knowledge and apparently were not modest about publicly proclaiming it.

It is interesting that the continuation of this story gives the reader a little hint that the Pharisees' Scriptural confidence was not as well founded as they believed. After they declared the crowd accursed, Nicodemus spoke up. He was a Pharisee, but he had secretly met with Jesus.[5] As discussed in the previous chapter, Jesus told Nicodemus in that meeting, "You are Israel's teacher and do you not understand these things?" after Nicodemus was incredulous about being "born again" and "born of the Spirit."[6] In this temple guard story, though, it was Nicodemus who is the more knowledgeable party:

> "Does our law condemn anyone without first hearing him to find out what he is doing?"[7]

The rest of the Pharisees answered with a snide retort:

> "Are you from Galilee, too? Look into it, and you will find that a prophet does not come out of Galilee."[8]

They failed to address Nicodemus' actual point and instead responded with an insult. What is particularly sad, though, is that having just insulted the mob's lack of Biblical knowledge, they responded to Nicodemus' critique with a statement that was Biblically wrong. There *were* prophets who arose from Galilee, including Jonah, Elijah, and Micah.[9] The Pharisees were either ignorant on that point or more interested in winning the argument than being Biblically correct.

One of the characteristics that Christians love most about themselves is that they are a people of the book. They love to invoke the Protestant Reformation's centerpiece *sola Scriptura*.[10] They are devoted to the Bible and they are experts in the Bible.

The Pharisees, as we have just seen, believed that about themselves as well. In Matthew 22, the writer shared a series of four encounters that Jesus had with the religious people of His day about their confidence in their Bible knowledge. This is a significant point: here we have four stories in a row all centered on the theme of Bible knowledge. Further, these four stories are found immediately before Matthew 23, the most essential Bible chapter for Jesus' condemnation of the Pharisees. The placement and four-fold repetition point to these being crucially important texts. As you might expect, it did not go well for the Pharisees and their religious allies.

As we look at these four stories, keep this thought in mind: the Pharisees were exceedingly proud of their Bible knowledge, but Jesus emphatically declared that their confidence was unfounded. Could the same accusation be made of Christians? If true, it would be a seismic blow that would strike at the very heart of Christian identity and confidence.

Give to Caesar

The first of the four is the well-known story of "give to Caesar what is Caesar's," which begins with two small but important details:

> Then the Pharisees went and plotted together how they might trap Him in what He said. And they sent their disciples to Him, along with the Herodians.[11]

The first detail reveals their intent in this encounter: that "they might trap Him." They were going to raise a Biblical issue intending to catch Jesus in His answer.

That leads us to the second detail: the Pharisees came to Jesus *with the Herodians*. To know why this is crucial, it is essential to understand the social dynamics of that day. The Pharisees and the Herodians were two of the major parties of the day. The Pharisees were strict in their observance of the Mosaic Law and passionate in their hope for the return of Israel to an independent nation (although not to the point of advocating violence like the Zealot party). The Herodians, as their name suggests, were in league with King Herod and the Romans who ruled Palestine. These two outlooks were diametrically opposed to each other. Specifically, the Pharisees believed that the Herodians were in bed with the devil and the Herodians believed the Pharisees were unrealistic about the actual situation in Israel. In sum, they were enemies.

This antagonism was what made it so telling that the two parties came *together* to confront Jesus. Both parties had reasons to want Jesus out of the way, since each in different ways had power within the existing system. In spite of their disdain for each other, they saw Jesus as the bigger threat and so in this moment they worked together.

The conspirators' plan was a simple one. They would go together and ask Jesus whether it was acceptable to pay taxes to Caesar. They presumed there were two possible answers. If Jesus answered, "Yes, pay the taxes" (Answer One), then the Pharisees would use that against Jesus with the throngs of people following Him. "See, this Jesus is just a patsy of the Roman occupation. He wants you to pay these oppressive taxes to this foreign occupier. You thought He was going to be your Messiah – well, that kind of weakness does not sound Messianic to us!"

On the other hand, if Jesus answered, "No, don't pay the taxes" (Answer Two), then the Herodians would take that information to the Roman rulers and tell them that Jesus was inciting rebellion. "This Jesus is telling the people that they do not have to pay their taxes. You had better deal with Him quickly and severely or you are going to have a rebellion on your hands."

It was a trap, just as the Bible text tells us. One answer led to losing His followers and therefore His power; the other led to being arrested by the Romans. It was a fool-proof plan.

Except for Jesus.

Jesus saw the trap and knew how to avoid it:

> But Jesus, knowing their evil intent, said, "You hypocrites, why are you *trying to trap [Me]*? Show me the coin used for paying the tax." They brought [Him] a denarius and [He] asked them, "Whose portrait is this? And whose inscription?" "Caesar's," they replied. Then [He] said to them, *"Give to Caesar what is Caesar's, and to God what is God's."* When they heard this, *they were amazed.*[12]

Their trap had failed.

Please remember that the focus of this chapter is on the Pharisees' use of the Bible. The point regarding that issue from this story is *the Pharisees used their Bible knowledge as a weapon to attempt to prove someone wrong.* (The Herodians did this as well, but we are focusing on the Pharisees.)

They came disguised as seekers of truth with a pointed Bible question. The issue they raised concerned the proper way to live out your faith in God as an Israelite. The Pharisees believed that the Bible promised them a Messiah who would lead them in throwing off the chains of foreign oppression. The Herodians, in contrast, believed that working with the Roman government was an acceptable way to live out their faith in God. They were not genuinely interested in knowing what Jesus had to say about the issue. They were not seeking insight for a fuller understanding of God. They were using their Bible knowledge with the sole intent of trapping Jesus in His answer toward discrediting and destroying Him. They were not interested in learning; they were interested in winning. *The Pharisees used their Bible knowledge as a weapon in an attempt to prove someone wrong.*

Examples abound of the Bible being used as a weapon within church life. In fact, it is rare to see two Christians who disagree on substantive theological points sit down, listen to the other's arguments, genuinely consider the other view, and then ask thoughtful and incisive questions in response. As has been said in another context, "Most people do not listen with the intent to understand; they listen with the intent to reply."[13] When Christians of different stripes talk, they use the Bible as a weapon. Among many who are well-versed in theology, they eagerly use the Bible to drive home their thoughts. In fact, it is considered a sign of spiritual maturity that you are adept at citing abundant proof texts and bringing forward incisive arguments to prove your point.

There is a caricature of Christians literally beating someone upside the head with a thick, leather-bound Bible. The caricature, like many, is not a whole cloth invention, but merely an exaggeration of a real, prominent trait. Winning a theological argument is a Christian joy. Putting people in their place with the Bible is just doing God's will and protecting the faith. Bible knowledge is about proving that my school of thought and I are right. It is about using my knowledge to win the argument. It is about catching that person in their wrongness. The Bible does refer to itself as the "sword of the Lord," but in most cases the way Christians use it results in blunt force trauma.[14]

In sum, this first story of "giving to Caesar" shows that *the Pharisees used their Bible knowledge as a weapon in an attempt to prove someone wrong*, just as Christians often do.[15]

Marriage at the Resurrection

The "giving to Caesar" confrontation is immediately followed by another Biblical argument – this time between Jesus and the Sadducees. This party of Jews was wealthier and more liberal than the Pharisees. Their key belief relevant to this discussion is that they did not believe in the resurrection of the dead.

The Sadducees approached Jesus with a Bible puzzle:

> "Moses told us that if a man dies without having children, his brother must marry the widow and have children for him. Now there were seven brothers among us. The first one married and died, and since he had no children, he left his wife to his brother. The same thing happened to the second and third brother, right on down to the seventh. Finally, the woman died. Now then, at the resurrection, whose wife will she be of the seven, since all of them were married to her?"[16]

Before getting to the more substantive matters, I should probably deal with your initial question: who in the world came up with the system of a widow marrying her brother-in-law? It is an Old Testament idea that just sounds weird to our Western ears. The dubious wisdom of such a system is an interesting question, but one that is unnecessary to the point I want to make in this chapter, so we will leave it for another day.

This was, to the minds of the Sadducees, an airtight theological argument: "You say there is going to be a resurrection of the dead someday, but if that is true then you end up with this woman being married to seven brothers![17] That is ridiculous and therefore proves there cannot be a resurrection of the dead." This little "seven brothers" story was their wonderfully constructed proof. It was their undeniable explanation. It was their knot no one could untie. In their mind, this example proved their case beyond any possible rebuttal.

Jesus, however, was not impressed. He replied:

> "You are in error because you do not know the Scriptures or the power of God."[18]

After the Sadducees confidently laid out their theological point, Jesus batted it aside. The key words He said were "You are in error." We will return to those in a moment.

Jesus elaborated on the Sadducees' error:

> "At the resurrection people will neither marry nor be given in marriage; they will be like the angels in heaven. But about the resurrection of the dead – have you not read what God said to you, 'I am the God of Abraham, the God of Isaac, and the God of Jacob'? He is not the God of the dead but of the living."[19]

Jesus made two points. The second one relied on verb tense. He reminded them that God said "I am the God of Abraham," not "I was the God of Abraham," which would have indicated that Abraham no longer existed.[20] The first one ("like the angels") conveyed a truth that was found nowhere in the Old Testament.

Jesus declared they "do not know . . . the power of God." There He was saying, "You all think that raising the dead would be too difficult, too big, too mind-boggling, but you do not understand how powerful God is and what He is able to accomplish."

More important for our purposes in this chapter is His statement that they "do not know the Scriptures." This section of the Bible, as I have shared, is focused on the understanding of Scripture. The last story ("give to Caesar") involved *the Pharisees using their Bible knowledge as a weapon in an attempt to prove someone wrong.* This section delivers a related point: *your confidence in your Bible knowledge is unfounded.* The heart of this story is Jesus' response to the Sadducees' airtight theological argument: "You are in error." The Sadducees gave their best theological argument to prove their point and Jesus straight up told them "you are wrong."

This "seven brothers" story was not one they had created for this situation. It was undoubtedly a well-worn Bible proof that had long impressed the Sadducee faithful with its power and wisdom. It gave them confidence in their Biblical understanding, yet Jesus casually swatted it away. Their confidence in their Bible knowledge was unfounded.

Do conservative Christians have great confidence in their Bible knowledge? Without question – none are more confident in their Bible knowledge. No one loves to argue the Bible more than conservative Christians. They have numerous airtight theological arguments. They have many wonderfully constructed proofs. They have countless undeniable explanations. They have a boxful of knots no one can untie.

Jesus hammers the Sadducees: *your confidence in your Bible knowledge is unfounded.* Is it possible He thinks the same of conservative Christians: *your confidence in your Bible knowledge is unfounded?* We have considered throughout this book whether conservative Christians are closely in line with God's will and found them lacking. Could it be they are not the Bible experts they think they are? If so, what a radical statement to consider for a people as uniformly proud and certain of their Bible knowledge as American conservative Christians.

Whose Son Is The Christ?

We now proceed to the fourth of the Matthew 22 stories about knowing the Scripture. (We will return to the third in a moment.) We find Jesus asking the Pharisees a Bible question:

Now while the Pharisees were gathered together, Jesus asked them a question: "What do you think about the Christ, whose son is He?"[21]

The Pharisees replied with the standard answer that the Christ (a.k.a. the Messiah) was the son of David.[22] By "son of David," they did not mean that He was literally one of David's sons, but rather that the Messiah would be one of the descendants of David. He would be of the lineage of David.[23] Jesus then posed His own Bible puzzle to them:

> "Then how does David in the Spirit call [the Christ] 'Lord,' saying, 'The Lord said to My Lord, "Sit at My right hand, until I put Your enemies beneath Your feet"'? If David then calls Him 'Lord,' how is He his son?"[24]

This is a complicated argument, but one that I will summarize as simply as I can. Jesus was essentially asking, "If the Christ is supposed to be the son of David, that obviously means that the Christ will come *after* David. You all know that in Jewish life we give great respect to our ancestors and honor them above ourselves. Further, we honor the heroes of our faith and none are greater than David. If David is both an ancestor to this Christ as well as a hero of the faith, then this Christ should be the one calling David 'Lord.' Yet the Scripture says that David is calling this Christ (who is one of his descendants) 'Lord.' Why would David give that high an honor to one of his descendants?"

The Pharisees have no answer:

> No one was able to answer Him a word, nor did anyone dare from that day on to ask Him another question.[25]

The answer that Jesus was looking for (and that the Pharisees did not know) was the miracle of the Incarnation. Jesus claimed to be the Christ and, even more dramatically, to be nothing less than the Incarnate Son of God – God in flesh. This was why David speaking "in the Spirit" (i.e. guided by the Holy Spirit to say something of which he did not understand the full implications) called the Christ "Lord." Yes, the Christ was coming after David, but the Christ deserved having the great David to call Him "Lord" because the Christ was the Incarnate Son of God.

The key phrase in this story is in the last verse: "No one was able to answer Him a word." Here is a core idea of the Old Testament and central tenet of the hope that the Pharisees held: the coming of the Christ, the arrival of the Messiah. Yet on this matter they have no answer to Jesus' question.

The central truth this story shares is this: *they were silent in the face of their real Bible knowledge.*

Christians, like most believers, focus their attention on the parts of the Bible they think they understand. They prefer to avoid the sections that push against the grain of their theology. They often maintain smugness about their Biblical understanding in part because they rarely leave the comfort of their favorite sections of Scripture.

Often Christians act as if they are the ones who have figured out the whole Bible. I argue that there is a zero percent chance of my standing before God someday and His telling me, "In all of human history, you are the one who perfectly figured out all the mysteries of the Bible!" Because of that, a great deal of humility is in order.

Christians love to talk about the Bible and share their interpretations. Is it possible that in the face of a question or two from Jesus (even on basic, core Scriptural issues) they too would be left in awkward, embarrassed silence, unable to even hazard a guess? Is it possible their confidence in their Bible knowledge is founded in their mastery of regurgitating their denomination's standard answers, an understanding that ignores many known questions and is sufficiently limited as to be unaware of even more mysteries? Is it possible that their confidence in their Bible knowledge is not a sign of Christlikeness, but cluelessness? The Pharisees, after all, were the party most passionate about the Law in their day, yet with one brief question about their greatest king and their greatest hope Jesus left them silent. Is it possible that Christians would fare similarly before Jesus? If so, why then are Christians so arrogant about their Bible knowledge?

What to Do With the Bible Then?

Let's take a moment to summarize our findings from Matthew 22 so far.

The first story was the "give to Caesar" interaction with the Pharisees and the Herodians. The central point made was *the Pharisees used their Bible knowledge as a weapon in an attempt to prove someone wrong.*

The second story was the "marriage at the resurrection" interaction with the Sadducees. The central point made was *their confidence in their Bible knowledge was unfounded.*

The fourth story was the "son of David" interaction with the Pharisees. The central point made was *they were silent in the face of their real Bible knowledge.*

Clearly it was Jesus' intent to disabuse the Pharisees (and the Sadducees and Herodians) of their overconfidence in their Bible knowledge. How do we respond to this, though? Do we throw the Bible out? Do we ignore it altogether?

This is where the third story becomes crucial. Unlike the other stories that highlight the errors that are being made by these groups, the third story points us to the right way to approach Scripture. It begins with what may be the biggest possible Bible question:

> Hearing that Jesus had silenced the Sadducees, the Pharisees got together. One of them, an expert in the law, tested [Him] with a question: "Teacher, which is the greatest commandment in the Law?"[26]

What is the core? Where should our focus be? What is the heart of the revelation of God? You know Jesus' reply:

> "'Love the Lord your God with all your heart and with all your soul and with all your mind.' This is the first and greatest commandment. And the second is like it: 'Love your neighbor as yourself.' All the Law and the

Prophets hang on these two commandments."²⁷

This is telling. In the midst of these three stories that point out the ways that the Pharisees' (and others') approach to the Bible yielded poor results, Jesus did not encourage them to double down and study more. He did not encourage them to expand their theology with more obscure details. He did not even demand a more rigorous schedule of Bible research and study. Instead, He pointed people to the two greatest commandments: love God and love your neighbor as yourself. The final phrase is the key one: "All the Law and the Prophets hang on these two commandments." If a person passionately pursues these two commandments, it puts them on a track for knowing the heart of the revelation of God.

How does this relate to the other three stories? This directs us toward a simple faith. It is one that is not focused on endless depths of obscure Bible trivia, but on becoming a person of deep love. It is one that does not look to the Bible for ammunition in an attempt to prove others wrong, but looks for insight to become increasingly loving. It is one that acknowledges that maturity is not about how much one knows, but how much one loves. It understands that loving God and loving others will not necessarily make a life easier, but it will make a life better and a heart fuller.

The key point is this: *it is not about hyped-up Bible knowledge, but lived-out love.* And the Pharisees' approach to the Bible did not lead to that type of love. Neither does Christians'. Allow me to repeat myself: despite their self-professed love for and expertise in the Bible, Christians' approach to the Scripture has not yielded the results God desires.

How is it that Christians have so many services to preach the Bible, yet live out so little love? How is that Christians have so many small group Bible studies, yet live out so little love? How is it that Christians have perhaps the most impressive array of Bible study resources ever assembled, yet live out so little love? How is it that Christians know so much about the Bible, yet are so quick to fight and argue in church? How is it that Christians have more time for Bible study than loving people? How is it that Christians are so proud to declare themselves people of the Word, yet are known by no one in our culture as people of love?

The point these four Matthew 22 stories direct us toward is that *the Bible improperly used becomes an impediment to a godly life*. It creates pride in the believer. It causes division within the church. It leads people away from a vibrant relationship with God.

The central question of this chapter is whether Christians are like the Pharisees in their approach to the Bible. The clear conclusion is that they are.

At this point, some of my Christian readers are screaming at this page. "There it is! He's abandoning the Scripture and telling everyone to just do what feels right! How can we know God's will unless we focus heavily on delving into the Bible? We will get horribly off track if the Bible is not the center of our faith."

Yet here in these stories we have multiple warnings. The Pharisees were slavishly focused on the Scripture and it did not lead them to fruitful lives. Centering on the Bible does not always lead to favorable outcome.

As painful as it is for Christians to admit, they must come back to the core understanding that Jesus is ultimately the Word of God, not the Bible. The very first words of the greatest gospel read, "In the beginning was the Word, and the Word was with God, and the Word was God."[28] That is not a reference to the Bible; it is a proclamation of Christ.

Think of the centuries before the printing press and yet millions were Christians despite not owning a Bible or even having an opportunity to read one. If everyday study of the Bible as the centerpiece of our faith lives was so essential, why did Christ come fourteen centuries before Gutenberg? Think of the millions of illiterate people today who are followers of Christ in spite of their inability to read.

While the Bible is a gift, making it the focus is a plan for a faith like the Pharisees'. It leads to endless parsing and debating. It leads to church splits and denominations perpetually subdividing into narrower and narrower emphases.

Nearing the end of His life, Jesus prayed in John 17 for a unified church[29]:

> "I pray . . . that all of them *may be one*."[30]

He further added that this unity among believers would be one of the church's most powerful witnesses to a disbelieving world:

> "May they be brought to complete unity to let the world know that [You] have sent [Me] and have loved them even as [You] have loved [Me]."[31]

Yet the Protestant church, so proud of being Bibliocentric, has been the worst violator of that hope in history, not so much in the initial break from Rome, but in the endless splintering into narrower and narrower denominations ever since.

The present approach leads to Christians "proving" their maturity, not with remarkable mercy or overwhelming love, but by being able to muster increasingly obscure minutiae to bolster their debates with other Christians. The most mature are those who can best win arguments, not win lost hearts.

The last thing most "three-services-a-week" Christians need is another Bible study. They are, spiritually speaking, morbidly obese and therefore horribly unhealthy. That spiritual "weight gain" comes from endless consumption of more and more Bible facts and trivia while all-too-rarely spiritually exercising. They have defined "faithful Christian" in a way that is heavily Bible centered: show up three times a week to listen to the Bible preached or taught and read a chapter of the Bible daily. There is less expectation of doing the hard work of service or character change. Under that system, it is the largest, rather than the fittest, believer who is considered the best Christian.

Does this mean Christians should throw the Bible away? No, but perhaps they should keep the big picture in sight. Jesus is ultimately the Word of God, not the Bible. The enemies of Jesus were overconfident – even arrogant – about their Biblical expertise. Jesus, in His interactions with them about that, pointed toward more humility, more awareness of how little they understood. They were not experts after all, according to Jesus. He further identified the centerpieces for following Him: love God, love your neighbor as yourself. Not complicated, but thoroughly life changing.

I am not arguing that the Bible is worthless. Far from it. Christians do need, though, to admit that they look like the Pharisees on this issue.

Over the last century and a half, the rise of Darwinism and Higher Criticism has created a cultural environment where Christians have felt forced to spend an inordinate amount of time "defending the Bible." Christianity became increasingly consumed with proving that the Bible still stood solid even in the face of powerful arguments to the contrary. As evangelicals and fundamentalists pushed inerrancy as a defense against those assaults, even more time and effort was required to defend the Bible, because inerrancy meant that any single proven mistake or contradiction in the Bible was sufficient to cause the whole house of cards to tumble.

Perhaps the focus was meant to be less on hard study of the small details of the Bible and more on the hard work of incorporating the big Jesus truths into hearts.

Consider the Bible over the last century and a half. Never has the Bible been more debated, never more studied, never more translated, never with more reference material available, never argued more passionately by the faithful that it is perfect and without blemish, and within that time none have been more passionate in those pursuits than conservative Christians. And yet. And yet as this book has established multiple times from various directions, the conservative Christian church today is decidedly and undeniably not Christlike. If more Bible was the problem, conservative Christians should be the greatest Christians in two millennia, yet there is no glimmer of hope that is remotely accurate. They have grasped their Bibles with two hands to proudly hold them high; in so doing has Christ slipped from their grasp?

Chapter Eight

"The Tradition of the Elders"

Fellowship dinners, C.E.O. pastors, and your Sunday best

Pastor Mark stepped out from behind the pulpit as he concluded his message. "And so society has completely thrown out the window all respect for the Sabbath. God clearly tells us here in the Ten Commandments that we are to keep the Sabbath Day holy, but all around us we see businesses open and kids' sports leagues going on like it is just another day. There is no respect for the Sabbath anymore! God gave it to us as a day of rest and worship. May we get back to that. Let us pray."

After the pastoral prayer, the congregation sang the invitation song. The youth pastor walked behind the pulpit to conclude the service as Pastor Mark walked to the back of the sanctuary to shake hands in a moment. "We again want to welcome all of you who are visiting today. Just a few quick reminders: there will be a Trustees' meeting immediately following service, the Easter play practice will begin at 3 p.m., choir practice is at 6 p.m., and evening service is at 7 p.m. God bless you all – this is the day that the Lord has made. Let's close in prayer."

Tradition and Commandment

The Jews followed the Old Testament Law, but the Pharisees took that a step further. As previously discussed, there was a host of additional rules they added to the already-lengthy Mosaic Law. The Pharisees felt the extra rules added clarity and specificity. Among the names they used to refer to these additional rules was "the tradition of the elders." The Pharisees saw these rules as binding.

In Mark 7 the Pharisees and Jesus have a little argument about the tradition of the elders. The Pharisees were upset that Jesus and His disciples were not following these traditions. The rule in question had to do with performing a ceremonial washing of hands before eating. The narrator explains:

> For the Pharisees and all the Jews do not eat unless they carefully wash their hands, thus observing *the traditions of the elders*; and when they come from the market place, they do not eat unless they cleanse themselves; and there are many other things which they have received in order to observe, such as the washing of cups and pitchers and copper pots.[1]

The Pharisees posed their concern to Jesus:

> The Pharisees and the scribes asked Him, "Why do Your disciples not walk according to *the tradition of the elders*, but eat their bread with impure hands?"[2]

The eating with "impure hands" would have been solved, in the Pharisees' eyes, by doing the proper ceremonial hand washing. In response, Jesus accused them of being hypocrites and then made this accusation:

> "Neglecting the commandment of God, you hold to the *tradition* of men."[3]

Jesus did not believe that the tradition of the elders was a means to better obey the Old Testament Law, but rather had the opposite effect:

> "You are experts at setting aside the commandment of God in order to keep your *tradition*."⁴

Jesus offered an example. In the Old Testament Law, God instructed the people of Israel to "honor your father and your mother."⁵ The tradition of the elders, though, provided a further "clarification":

> [Jesus] was also saying to them, . . . "Moses said, 'Honor your father and your mother,' . . . but you say, 'If a man says to his father or his mother, whatever I have that would help you is Corban (that is to say, given to God),' you no longer permit him to do anything for his father or his mother; thus invalidating the word of God by your tradition which you have handed down; and you do many things such as that."⁶

The accusation was straightforward: the Pharisees failed to obey the commands of God because they obeyed the tradition of the elders. Rather than helping the Jewish people to obey the Mosaic Law, the traditions of the elders as lived out by the Pharisees in fact often stood in the way of obeying the Old Testament Law. In this case, the original Law had clearly stated that they were to honor their parents; the tradition of the elders, though, created a situation where it was acceptable to declare the resources that would have been used for that purpose as dedicated to God.

Why would someone do that? We cannot be sure, but perhaps it happened something like this. Someone did not have sufficient money to pay their obligations to the Temple and to their parents. The rabbis were consulted about which should have priority. Obviously, God is more important than anything else, so presumably the financial obligation to God was foremost. Over time, that idea became codified into the rules in the form that Jesus explained. However it happened, the fundamental point was obvious: the rules that had been made to "help" people follow God were actually getting in the way of obeying God's commandments.

Christians' Tradition of the Elders

Christians do not have anything that they specifically call the "tradition of the elders." Nonetheless, do they commit similar sins that the Pharisees did? Do their religious rules sometimes stand in the way of people obeying God's commandments? The answer is yes. I will share several examples to prove my point.

1. Church membership.

How often in the New Testament is the word "member" used to refer to someone who has his name on a church roll? The answer: zero. Instead, it is used as part of an analogy: each Christian is like a "member" (that is, a part) of a spiritual body. The church as a whole is the "body," with Christ as its head. In that thought, each Christian within that congregation is a "member" of that body:

> For the body is not one *member*, but many.[7]

> But now God has placed *members*, each one of them, in the body, just as He desired. If they were all one *member*, where would the body be? But now there are many *members*, but one body.[8]

Each part of the body is called a "member" of the body. The importance of the analogy is in the active working of each *member*. If someone has an ear that is not working, that causes problems for the person. If someone has a liver that does not do its job, that causes problems for the person. If this spiritual body has "members" that are not working that causes problems for the body as a whole.

In church life, though, being a "member of the church" means something different from the Biblical definition. It means that a person expressed his desire to join a congregation and his name was entered on the church roll as a "member" of that congregation. No further activity required; no additional work necessary. In fact, most congregations have a "membership" that is two or three times larger than the actual number of people attending on a typical Sunday.

The practical problem with this is it diminishes expectations of what it means to be a part of the body of Christ. I can be a "member" of the church and not even show up. This is a choice that Christians have made in defining membership. They could alter their definition so that only those actively serving in a ministry are considered members. They could simply dispense with the idea of people coming forward to "join" a church. Instead, they uniformly define membership in this skewed manner. This Christian "tradition of the elders" gets in the way of people having a proper Biblical understanding of what it means to be a part of a church (a "member" of the "body").

2. Wearing your Sunday best.

Although clothing standards have become more lax generally in American society over the last twenty years, everyone still knows what is meant by "wearing your Sunday best." It has long been a tradition in American churches to wear your finest clothes to church. This is a tradition that is encouraged by many Christians because they see it as a sign of respect for God. "God is worthy of your best," they will say, so you should walk into the sanctuary wearing the best you have to offer. Certainly today there are numerous exceptions with more contemporary churches emphasizing casual attire, but a trip to any restaurant at 1 p.m. on Sunday will clearly show that a lot of Christians still dress up for church.

The problem is that fancy clothes are apparently not what God wants. In one of the few New Testament passages on clothing, Paul wrote:

> I . . . want the women to dress modestly, with decency and propriety, adorning themselves, not with elaborate hairstyles or gold or pearls

> or expensive clothes, but with good
> deeds, appropriate for women who
> profess to worship God.⁹

This passage is not written specifically regarding church apparel, but what women should generally wear. It naturally follows, though, that if God does not want showy clothing and accessories throughout the week, it would not make much sense for Him to suddenly want women wearing such things to come and worship Him. Although this passage does not specifically address men's clothing, I presume the same principle is in play. This, of course, flows right along with Jesus' teaching that what is within a person matters most:

> "on the outside you appear to people
> as righteous but on the inside you are
> full of hypocrisy and wickedness."¹⁰

What does this mean? It means that Christians' long-standing encouragement for their people to "wear their Sunday best" is a man-made rule that serves to cause them to violate the actual command of God to be modest in dress. Thus Christians' version of the "tradition of the elders" does the same thing that Jesus accused the Pharisees of doing.

3. The church building.

How often in the New Testament is the word "church" used to refer to a building? Answer: zero. In every instance it refers to a body of believers rather than a brick-and-mortar structure. The early church had no buildings – they usually met in smaller groups in people's homes. Modern Christians, though, not only have church buildings, but largely have no vision of a church family that does not *require* a building (preferably a big one!). In fact, some of the Christians reading this had no idea that you even *could* have a body of believers without a building.

The pursuit of a large congregation meeting in one place (as opposed to smaller group meeting in homes) is a choice Christians have made that has practical consequences. Two of those: 1. Most congregations spend an embarrassing percentage of their budgets on constructing and maintaining their building. It is not unusual for one-third to one-half of the money donated to the church to be spent on the building. 2. The decision to pursue a large body of believers all meeting in one place often requires a full-time pastor (preferably seminary trained). After all, if you are going to have that large a congregation, you need someone well trained to lead. Someone in such a position deserves a fair wage and benefits. This too creates a substantial financial burden on the body of believers.

My point here is not to condemn church buildings per se or to say that full-time pastors are intrinsically evil. (After all, I have been a full-time pastor for much of my time in ministry). My point is that those are choices of how to do ministry. You are not required to have a church building to be a church. It is a choice of approaches, and one with consequences. You are not required to have a large number of believers meeting in one place who require a full-time pastor. It is a choice of approaches, and one with consequences.

Spending money on one thing (a building, for example) intrinsically means that money cannot be spent on something else. A case can be made that spending such large percentages of the church budget on buildings and pastoral salaries is diverting funds from more Biblically sound expenses.

A couple passages to consider. In Galatians 2, Paul told the story of meeting the apostles and convincing them that God had opened up a door for him to minister to the Gentiles (the non-Jewish people).[11] After he had convinced them, they sent Paul and his companion Barnabas off to preach the gospel. As he went, they requested one thing of Paul:

> They only asked us to remember the poor – the very thing I also was eager to do.[12]

This is such a critical moment in church history as Paul and Barnabas go out to minister to the Gentiles while Peter and the rest of the apostles go out to minister to the Jews. In that moment, one thing they both agreed needed to be prioritized as they shared the gospel was "remember the poor."

In Matthew 25, Jesus speaks of Final Judgment and how the judge will separate the "sheep" from the "goats." What is the standard that will be used?

> "Come, you who are blessed of My Father, inherit the kingdom prepared for you from the foundation of the world. For I was hungry, and you gave Me something to eat; I was thirsty, and you gave Me something to drink; I was a stranger, and you invited Me in; naked, and you clothed Me; I was sick, and you visited Me; I was in prison, and you came to Me."[13]

They wonder when they have done that to Him and He replies what they did to "even the least of them, you did it to Me."[14] What a Christian does to the least of the people around her is what she does to Jesus.

These two passages taken together make a clear point: Jesus expects His people to care for the poor. This does not merely mean to have emotional compassion for the poor, but to provide practical financial help for them in their time of need (food, water, clothes, medicine, just to name the ones enumerated in Matthew 25). While there are obviously numerous Christian ministries who are helping the poor, an honest assessment cannot help but conclude that the efforts are underwhelming. Most churches spend a mere ten percent of their income on "missions," with much of that going to missionaries and usually some smaller percentage going to such helping ministries. Stated differently, the vast majority of American churches are spending at least 90 percent of their income on themselves, with a pittance going to foreign, national, and local ministries that happen outside the walls of their church. They do this because the bulk of their budget is already claimed by building and pastoral salary expenses.

Just consider this thought for a moment: what if every congregation in America was structured in a way that allowed them to give 50 percent of their income away to help people in the community? It is possible – it is just not the structure that they have chosen. Instead, the Christian "tradition of the elders" teaches that any decent church is going to have its own building. Additionally, the Christian "tradition of the elders" teaches that a successful church will have a full-time pastor (or even better, multiple staff). Those two traditions block American churches from being able to obey the Biblical commands to help the poor to the extent that they otherwise could.

One final thought on this subject before moving on. A particularly despicable accusation that Jesus made against the Pharisees was that they "devour widows' houses."[15] The phrase conjures thoughts of unscrupulously taking for their own benefit some of the sparse resources those poor women had. The sympathetic image of frail, vulnerable older women reverberates in one's heart. A provocative question: could it be that Christians are also "devouring widow's houses" today?

Early in the book of Acts, the first deacons were commissioned.[16] There was a daily distribution of food within the church and it kept the apostles from their preaching and praying, so they choose some reputable men to handle that ministry. The important point here is that *there was a daily distribution of food*. That is to say, the church was attending to the practical needs of the poor widows within the church (the widows are specifically mentioned in Acts 6).[17]

Today it is often the elderly within the church who are the most faithful to give their tithes and offerings. This includes many widows on fixed incomes who can scarcely afford to give to the church but do nonetheless. Most churches depend on those funds to pay their expenses. In the modern conservative Christian church, however, the majority of church income goes toward expenses like pastoral salary and the church building, with almost no money spent to attend to the practical needs of people within or outside the church.

Could an argument be made that church leaders are using widows' funds to help bankroll a version of church that returns no practical benefit to those widows? Could an argument be made that doing so is "devouring widows' houses"? That is, that they are using widows' funds to further their religious structures rather than having the care of the widow as the primary concern. Rather than being a part of God's mercy and supply into the widows' lives, are Christians looking to *widows' houses* as a resource they can utilize to meet their budget without having to give anything in return? If so, it would be a devastating indictment of the church.

The larger point is that it is a Christian "tradition of the elders" to have a building, despite the lack of Biblical evidence for the necessity of one. This choice consumes much of the church budget that might otherwise go to more Biblical priorities like caring for the poor. I write this understanding that many Christians reading these words attend a church with a building. Of the three churches I have pastored, two have been traditional churches with buildings.[18] Even in such situations, work can still be done to maximize the amount of money going to ministry instead of maintenance.[19] Still, the larger point holds that current church spending is rarely focused on Biblical priorities.

4. Pastoral career path.

The career path of most pastors looks eerily similar to the career path of most Americans: passionately pursuing the bigger, better, more lucrative opportunity. Pastors move from smaller churches to larger ones. If a pastor moves from a church of five hundred to a church of seventy-five, the first question that the other pastors in his ministerial association will ask is, "What went wrong?" You just do not do that. You are always supposed to be moving up.

Two passages are worth mentioning with regard to this. One is from Paul in the opening chapter of 1 Corinthians:

> God has chosen the weak things of
> the world to shame the things which
> are strong.[20]

It is a reminder that God likes choosing things that are unimpressive by human standards through which to work. So often He chose obscure places ("Can any good thing come out of Nazareth?"[21]) and the least impressive person (when Samuel went to discern which son of Jesse would be the new king, they did not even bother to bring David in for the line-up[22]). God did that so that when the victory came it would be clear that His power brought it to pass. Given that repeated pattern in the Bible, should there not be a desire to be in some of the smaller or more obscure places in order to see God's power manifested?

Further, Jesus was clear about the dangers of striving to put oneself in a higher position:

> "For everyone who exalts himself will
> be humbled, and he who humbles
> himself will be exalted."[23]

This again points toward a willingness to take the lesser place and then allow the power of God to flow through that humility in order to see effective ministry.

Too often pastors have limited what God can do through them within their roles as pastors by choosing their pastorates based on the world's rules of corporate rung-climbing. Some will counter that more experienced pastors need to be in larger churches because they are better able to run those ministries. That does not wash, though. We are looking for the greatest movement of God we can get, not the most efficient organizing of the work force. Within pastoral circles, there is a clear expectation that good pastors will move to continually larger congregations. That "tradition of the elders" limits what God can do by frustrating the positioning of gifted people that He would prefer.

5. Church growth.

If you ask a Christian which churches in his town are the most successful, those named will almost without fail have one thing in common: drawing a big crowd. When a church is searching for a new pastor, one of the desires that is almost always near the top of their "wish list" is someone who can "grow the church." If a Christian publication is looking for someone to quote, they will inevitably seek out the pastor of a megachurch, because that is presumed to be someone who is a successful pastor.

In one respect, a large church can obviously be a good thing if it is filled with genuinely saved and transformed believers. More often, though, large congregations can point in a different direction.

Specifically, it can teach that drawing a crowd is the primary goal of the church.

This cuts against some key Scripture. First, Jesus stated that the path to salvation was not heavily trod:

> "Enter through the narrow gate. For wide is the gate and broad is the road that leads to destruction, and many enter through it. But small is the gate and narrow the road that leads to life, and only a few find it."[24]

This is a clear indication that having a large crowd does not intrinsically mean that you are on the right path.

Second, Jesus Himself had moments of great popularity with people, but found that in the end His teaching drove many away:

> From this time many of [His] disciples turned back and no longer followed [Him]. "You do not want to leave too, do you?" Jesus asked the Twelve.[25]

Again, a reminder that sometimes sharing the truth does not bring a bigger crowd.

Third, and perhaps most importantly, this emphasis that the church's main goal is bigger attendance on Sunday morning easily distracts the leadership and the congregation from the more important goal, which is growing believers into Christlikeness:

> This will continue until we all come to such unity in our faith and knowledge of God's Son that we will be mature in the Lord, measuring up to the full and complete standard of Christ.[26]

The focus of the local church should be less on having a large crowd on Sunday morning and more on growing people into Christlikeness. When this is actually pursued, there will almost certainly be folks drawn to the church, as genuine Christlikeness is intrinsically attractive. But when the crowd is pursued as the main goal and not as a possible side effect of effective evangelism and discipleship, the likelihood of congregations that are a mile wide and an inch deep becomes prevalent.

If you ask someone who is a part of a struggling church looking for new leadership what they are hoping to find, the inevitable answer will be "someone who can grow our church." Notice the focus there. It is not on people being saved and transformed. It is not on maturity into Christlikeness. The focus is avoiding the demise of the church in which they are emotionally invested. To that line of thinking, people being saved or growing into Christlikeness are merely means to the end of preserving their beloved church.

Christians focus passionately on church growth and in that pursuit many times put secondary things first. The church growth "tradition of the elders" leaves them with flagship congregations that often are impressive in breadth, but not depth.

6. Wednesday night prayer meeting.

Most conservative Christian churches have a "Wednesday night prayer meeting." This usually consists of an opening song, prayer requests from the congregation followed by prayer, and then a Bible study from the pastor. It is standard evangelical fare.

If you attend one of these meetings, you will notice something about the prayer requests that are verbally received from the congregation. Ninety-nine percent of them are about physical problems. "Uncle Harry is having open heart. Pray for him." "My wife is still struggling with her breathing. Continue to lift her up." "We need to keep praying for Margie and her radiation treatments."

Now, obviously, lifting people's physical needs up in prayer is not a bad thing. It is usually born of genuine concern for people. (Although, to be honest, with some in the congregation, it arises from a desire to share a little gossip.) The problem is that *physical* prayer requests are the overwhelming bulk of what is offered. Generally, the only time this varies is if the pastor makes it a point to specifically ask for unsaved people for whom to pray, at which time a few names will be offered.

It must be remembered that people are learning about prayer in those meetings. Not just about how to pray, but also about what to pray. And what they are learning is that you should spend most of your prayer time on physical needs.

It is notable that some of the greatest intercessory prayers in the New Testament have to do with *spiritual* issues. Paul shared eloquent prayers for spiritual maturity in several of his letters:

> I keep asking that the God of our Lord Jesus Christ, the glorious Father, may give you the Spirit of wisdom and revelation, so that you may know [Him] better. I pray that the eyes of your heart may be enlightened in order that you may know the hope to which [He] has called you, the riches of [His] glorious inheritance in [His] holy people, and [His] incomparably great power for us who believe.[27]

> With this in mind, we constantly pray for you, that our God may make you worthy of [His] calling, and that by [His] power [He] may bring to fruition your every desire for goodness and your every deed prompted by faith. We pray this so that the name of our Lord Jesus may be glorified in you, and you in [Him], according to the grace of our God and the Lord Jesus Christ.[28]

Jesus also prayed for spiritual needs:

> "I do not ask You to take [the disciples] out of the world, but to keep them from the evil one . . . . Sanctify them in the truth; Your word is truth."[29]

What is noteworthy here is that Paul and Jesus prayed for the spiritual growth and maturity of *believers*. On Wednesday evenings, if a spiritual prayer request is offered, it is inevitably for an unsaved person to find Christ. The praying by believers for their fellow believers to grow in spiritual maturity is simply nonexistent.

The "tradition of the elders" in these churches is to have many physical concerns raised in prayer on Wednesday evenings. Doing so points people away from praying for the more important and lasting concern: people's spiritual growth.

7. Pastor's role.

Many Christians see the pastor as the person who is hired to "run the church." Most congregations want someone who can get things moving and lead the church to growth. The pastoral role is often seen as similar to the C.E.O. of a business.

In contrast, there is an important scene early in Acts that gives clear definition to the pastoral role. The apostles found themselves unable to get everything done and so they decided to appoint the first deacons to handle some of the practical necessities (in this case, the distribution of food to the widows).[30] They appointed seven men to handle this task so that they could attend to the pastoral role:

> "But we will devote ourselves to prayer and to the ministry of the word."[31]

In other words, the two things that the church leaders were supposed to be focusing their time and attention on were (a) prayer and (b) preaching.

Most pastors spend a decent amount of time on preaching, but then again that is something that has a public aspect to it. (You can only fake being prepared to preach so many times before it catches up with you.) Prayer, though, is another matter.

When Jesus threw tables in the Temple because of the corruption there, He proclaimed:

> "It is written, 'My house shall be called a *house of prayer*'; but you are making it a robbers' den."[32]

There are a host of good words He could have chosen there. "My house shall be called a house of grace." "A house of evangelism." "A house of the Spirit." But among all those, He apparently most wanted His house to be a house of prayer. That was one reason why He wanted His pastors to make prayer one of the two main things on which they focused.

Congregations will say that they want their pastor to be a person of prayer, but their churches are too heavily scheduled for that to be a practical reality. They will say they want to be guided by prayer, but they resist the call to wait on God. ("We need to get things moving.") They will say they believe in the power of prayer, but then everything they do presumes that they have to make it happen themselves.

The Bible proclaims that one of the two things that pastors should focus their time on is prayer, but the "tradition of the elders" in Christian circles is built to have the pastor too busy to actually spend a substantial amount of time in prayer. Unlike preaching, prayer is private in nature and can be neglected without an immediate indication. Certainly, a church with a prayer-less pastor will be a church without power, but the private nature of prayer will keep the congregation from knowing that the pastor is part of the problem.

8. Worship as performance.

The typical evangelical church service can feel like a performance. There is a stage up front where everyone is to focus their attention. The "performers" – the pastor, the soloist, the choir, the person sharing the morning prayer – ascend to the stage to share their aspect of the service. The people see themselves as a passive audience. During the service, the most they add is a spoken "Amen" and their combined voices to the congregation singing. It is after worship, though, that they fulfill their function: judging the quality of the performance. "I got a lot out of that." "That was boring." "She was off-key." The thought rarely crosses their minds that they are not the audience, but rather are meant to also be participants in worship with God as the audience.

There is an interesting verse in 1 Corinthians 14:

> What then shall we say, brothers and sisters? When you come together, each of you has a hymn, or a word of instruction, a revelation, a tongue or an interpretation. Everything must be done so that the church may be built up.[33]

There would obviously be disagreement between Baptists and Pentecostals whether speaking in tongues and interpreting is still operative for today, but the larger principle remains: Paul was teaching them here that each of them were to bring something to worship to share. Of course, back in that day, the churches were not meeting in large halls, but in homes, so the groups were smaller. Still, it was a participatory worship, with each one bringing something.

What might that look like today? Perhaps one brings a song to sing. Another sings just a verse from a song that has been on her heart all week. Several share a testimony or praise of something that happened to them that week. A few more talk about a verse that jumped out to them in their Bible reading for that week. Three share short sermons they have prepared from the Bible. (Many of you are wondering why it would not just be the main pastor sharing the thirty-minute sermon. Well, that thirty-minute sermon is nowhere in the New Testament. It does not specify how long the pastor is to preach. Further, in several of the New Testament passages, when it speaks of those leading the church, it uses the plural, indicating that there was not necessarily one designated pastor but several people who were leading.[34]) Most of those in the room participate, having come with something to share with their brothers and sisters in Christ. Obviously, this would work better with a smaller congregation.

This, of course, is unlike what you will find in almost any American evangelical church. It must be said that the default pattern of worship in Christian churches is not one specified by the Bible. It is a comfortable format, long used, but as this verse indicates it may well be that the "tradition of the elders" when it comes to order of worship cuts against the joyful sharing that the New Testament specifically requested.

9. **The Sabbath rest.**

Most churches have a full calendar. It is taken as a sign of the spiritual vibrancy of the congregation. "We have a lot going on here!" No day is more packed with events and activities than Sunday. It might look something like this: Sunday School at 10 A.M.; morning worship at 11 A.M.; Christian Education committee meeting at 6 P.M.; evening worship at 7 P.M.; choir practice at 8 P.M. If you are counting, that is five hours in the church building. Certainly this is not true of every believer, but for those who are make up the core of the church it is not extraordinary.

The weekly Sabbath day was intended to have two purposes: worship and rest. With all the pressing moral concerns that could have been included in the Ten Commandments, a Sabbath rest was considered important enough to make it:

> "Remember the Sabbath day by keeping it holy. Six days you shall labor and do all your work, but the seventh day is a Sabbath to the Lord your God. On it you shall not do any work, neither you, nor your son or daughter, nor your male or female servant, nor your animals, nor any foreigner residing in your towns. For in six days the Lord made the heavens and the earth, the sea, and all that is in them, but [He] rested on the seventh day. Therefore the Lord blessed the Sabbath day and made it holy."[35]

This makes it clear that there should be a weekly day of rest. There is much to be said about Christians not slowing down at all outside of church on Sundays – it is just another day of chores, errands, and busyness – but that is a subject outside of our immediate concern. That concern is that church leaders have pushed aside the idea of the Sabbath as a day of rest in favor of the Sabbath as a day of church activity. This is the "tradition of the elders" that directly contradicts the Bible's clear teaching, yet it is business as usual in almost every conservative Christian church.

10. A personal relationship with Jesus.

The ubiquitous conservative Christian description for being a Christian is "having a personal relationship with God." It arises from an admirable source: the truth that you cannot rely on someone else's faith (perhaps a mother or father, spouse or child) to make you right with God. Each person must individually make her peace with God. "Having a personal relationship with God" is so common that most Christians would be shocked to know that the phrase appears nowhere in the Bible.

The problem with the "tradition of the elders" of describing salvation as "having a personal relationship with God" is that it seriously obscures what that salvation is to be. The central problem is this: salvation is understood as something that merely requires an acquaintance with Jesus, not obedience to the teaching of Jesus. Someone might ask me if I have a personal relationship with Mike. Perhaps I have not seen Mike in five years, but we did know each other at one point, so my answer to the question is "yes." We see this repeatedly in spiritual lives with people who rarely give God the slightest thought and make no effort to follow the teaching of Christ nonetheless claiming to "have a personal relationship with Jesus" because they were baptized as a teen or went forward at a revival years ago. Christians' repeated use of this phrase to characterize salvation leads people to believe that they are in good standing with God because they "have a personal relationship with God."

In truth, one of the Biblical expectations for a Christian is obedience to the teachings of Christ. Because I have dealt with this subject earlier in this book, I will limit myself to two examples:

> Jesus . . . said to him, "*Follow Me!*"
> And he got up and followed Him.[36]

> "Not everyone who says to Me, 'Lord, Lord,' will enter the kingdom of heaven, but *he who does the will of my Father.*"[37]

The first speaks to Jesus' desire for *followers*. He called *disciples* to Himself. The second notes that *obedience* to the teaching of Christ is necessary. In both cases, the life of faith is envisioned as a life of living out the teaching of Jesus, rather than an empty admiration of Christ or a claim of a "relationship" that leaves one's life unchanged. Christians' "tradition of the elders" of consistently referring to "having a relationship with Jesus" discourages people from understanding the nature of saving faith and undertaking life as an apprentice of Jesus.

Conclusion

Jesus rebuked the Pharisees for the way they put their "tradition of the elders" foremost:

> "You are experts at setting aside the commandment of God in order to keep your tradition . . . . [You are] invalidating the word of God by your tradition which you have handed down; and you do many things such as that."[38]

Do Christians do the same thing - pursuing their "tradition of the elders" even when it leads God's people to do things contrary to the Word of God? Yes, and repeatedly.

Amazingly, a typical Christian would be more incensed by someone trying to change one of these traditions than they are that those very traditions are causing them to disobey God. Don't believe me? Go into a conservative Christian congregation, try to change one of the examples I have shared in this chapter, and watch the resistance.

Chapter Nine

"Lovers of Money"

Consumerism, greed, and America's greatest sin

A young mother and her seven-year-old son pulled into the church parking lot with only a couple minutes until Sunday School. She grabbed the wallet out of her purse as he unbuckled his seatbelt. All she had in there was a dollar and a quarter, so she grabbed them both and handed them to her son.

As they got out of the car and walked in, her son looked at the money and asked, "Mom, do you want me to put both in the plate in Ms. Becky's class?" A smile came across the mom's face and she replied, "I tell you what – you put one in and you can keep one. Ok?" "All right," he said as he looked down at the money in his hands, "but which one?"

"You choose," she answered.

Sunday School and church went fine. They were back home sitting down to eat grilled cheese for lunch when the mom remembered the offering money. "I forgot to ask you," she said. "What did you put in the offering plate in class?"

Her son put down his grilled cheese and dug down in his pocket. He pulled out the dollar bill and laid it on the table.

"Why did you give the quarter instead of the dollar?" she asked.

"Well, I remembered that you told me last week that God loves a cheerful giver and I figured that I'd be happier if I still had the dollar."

The desire to keep more for oneself and to spend more on oneself is a basic human tendency. This is heightened in a country like America that enjoys such material prosperity. The question for this chapter is how that natural bent toward loving money and possessions plays out in the lives of American Christians.

Wealth as a Sign of Divine Favor

A young man with extraordinary wealth approached Jesus to ask about possessing eternal life. Jesus shared some challenging words with him, which caused him to walk away discouraged, unwilling to make financial sacrifices.[1] Jesus then told those around Him:

> "How hard it is for those who are wealthy to enter the kingdom of God! For it is easier for a camel to go through the eye of a needle than for a rich man to enter the kingdom of God."[2]

This stunned the crowd. They asked incredulously, "Then who can be saved?"[3]

This question tells us much about the expectations of Jesus' listeners concerning the wealthy. In that day, the prevailing thought was that wealth was a sign of divine favor. Those who were wealthy were presumed to be blessed by God and therefore at the front of the heavenly line. Jesus clearly had a different mentality.

Jesus expounded upon this thought in Luke 16, which will be the primary focus of this chapter. There He made several controversial statements about money, which led the Pharisees to "scoff" at Him.[4] Why were they so negative? Luke tells us the reason:

> Now the Pharisees, who were *lovers of money*, were listening to all these things and were scoffing at Him.[5]

This tells us something central about the Pharisees, which is a little surprising at first. One might presume that a people so religious would be above such material things. I think their love of money largely arose from the idea that wealth was a sign of divine blessing. Their money therefore became an outward indication of God's favor on their life.

The next verse points in this direction:

> And He said to them, "You are those who justify yourselves in sight of men, but God knows your hearts."[6]

The entire passage is about money, so the idea here of justifying yourself means finding confirmation of divine favor through your money. Whatever the root cause, consider the fundamental point: the Pharisees were lovers of money.

We are going to unpack Jesus' money statements here in Luke 16, each of which stand in opposition to the Pharisees' love of money. After digging in, we will consider whether American Christians are guilty in similar ways.

A Parable That Seems to Excuse Treachery

Luke 16 begins with one of Jesus' most perplexing parables. It is confounding because an initial reading seems to excuse dubious behavior. It begins with a manager getting canned:

> "There was a rich man who had a manager, and this manager was reported to him as squandering his possessions. And he called him and said to him, 'What is this I hear about you? Give an accounting of your management, for you can no longer be manager.'"[7]

This obviously put the manager in a tough situation:

> "What shall I do, since my master is taking the management away from

me? I am not strong enough to dig; I am ashamed to beg.'"[8]

He knew the loss of his job was imminent, so he acted quickly:

> "'I know what I shall do, so that when I am removed from the management people will welcome me into their homes.' And he summoned each one of his master's debtors, and he began saying to the first, 'How much do you owe my master?' And he said, 'A hundred measures of oil.' And he said to him, 'Take your bill, and sit down quickly and write fifty.' Then he said to another, 'And how much do you owe?' And he said, 'A hundred measures of wheat.' He said to him, 'Take your bill, and write eighty.'"[9]

He called in his master's debtors and renegotiated what they owed, making their balance more favorable to them. ("You owe a hundred? How about if we change that to fifty?") This obviously would make it more likely that someone would welcome him when he shortly found himself out of work. It is pretty smart, but it is also – let's admit it – a little sneaky. It sounds devious.

Now comes the shocker. Remember that this was a parable that Jesus told, so this was His story. After telling of the manager renegotiating his master's debts, Jesus closed out the story with this:

> "And the master *praised the unrighteous servant* because he had acted *shrewdly*."[10]

What? This parable ends with the manager being the hero instead of the culprit? What kind of sense does that make? Because of that difficulty, many Bible commentators do not know what to do with this parable. They are embarrassed by it. In truth, though, there is nothing of which to be ashamed. The key is the next verse.

Jesus brought out the point of application for the listener:

> "for the sons of this age are more shrewd in relation to their own kind than the sons of light. And I say to you, *make friends for yourself by means of the wealth of unrighteousness, so that when it fails, they will receive you into the eternal dwellings.*"[11]

Jesus was not praising the manager's deviousness; He was praising his shrewdness. The manager used the financial resources that were available to him (in this case, his master's) to accomplish his aim (in this case, employment). Remember that this is in a Bible chapter that is focused on the subject of money, so the point here is also financially centered. I would summarize Jesus' point in this way: *use what you control to accomplish your goal*. For the manager, it played out this way: he still had control of his master's financial books and he used them to bring about the goal of a new job for himself. He was *shrewd in his use of that money* because he used it in a focused way to bring about what he wanted.

What behavior did Jesus want to see in His followers as a result of this parable? Again, we are talking about money, so Jesus was telling His followers that He wanted them to be shrewd in how they used their financial resources. He told them to "make friends for yourself" by using your money ("by means of the wealth of unrighteousness"). Knowing the larger context of Jesus' desire for those who are lost to come into the Kingdom of God (see, most poignantly, all of Luke 15), I believe what He was saying here was along the lines of this: use your financial resources to invest in people, to show them genuine love when they are struggling, to show them the compassion of God in caring for their needs, with the prayer that your "investment" will help them to appreciate God's love for them through you and that they will be drawn to God. The cross teaches Jesus' followers that what matters most is people. Use your financial resources, Jesus is teaching, to show God's love to those around you.

That leads to Jesus' stated goal:

> "so that when [the money] fails, [those friends] will receive you into the eternal dwellings."

I would paraphrase it something like this: if your passion and heart are to see people experience the love of God in their lives, when you come to the end of your life and all that money cannot be taken with you to the other side, those people who have died before you who were drawn closer to God through your love shown through your money will be there in eternity to welcome you and let you know with certainty that you invested your money well when you invested it in pointing people toward God's love. To return to my summary statement: use what you control to accomplish your goal. "What you control" in this context is the financial resources that flow through your life; "accomplish your goal" in this context for the follower of Jesus should be people drawn closer to God in salvation or maturity. The overall point Jesus was going for was that *He wanted His followers to focus their money ambitions on pointing people toward His Father.* One presumes that Jesus understood the need for food, clothing, and shelter, but wanted to encourage His followers to spend as lavishly as possible on what matters most to His heart: people loving His Father. Thus the point of the parable is not about deviousness but about the manager's shrewd focus on accomplishing his goal. Jesus was encouraging His followers to be *shrewd* in how they spend their money: make sure you spend your money on what will accomplish your goal (and your goal should be people knowing God).

Understood in this way, this parable stands as a harsh condemnation of the modern American church's wholesale acceptance and pursuit of an increasingly higher standard of living while all around them people flounder in lives without God. American Christians are rarely focused on passionately spending their financial resources to see people know God; they are, however, regularly focused on passionately spending their financial resources to see themselves enjoy the American Dream. We will return to this later.

Money Is a Test

Some may be willing to concede the point that American Christians are not putting their financial resources on Kingdom goals to the extent that they should be. However, they will counter, at least it is only money and not something spiritually significant. Unfortunately for such thinking, the two verses that immediately follow the shrewd manager parable speak to the contrary.

In Luke 16:10-11, Jesus continued:

> "He who is faithful in a very little thing is faithful also in much; and he who is unrighteous in a very little thing is unrighteous also in much. Therefore if you have not been faithful in the use of unrighteous wealth, who will entrust the true riches to you?"[12]

Jesus first established the principle that how well you handle a small matter indicates how well you would handle a large matter. This is a truth that can be applied to many aspects of life, but Jesus immediately pointed it back to money. He asked how God could entrust true riches to a person who had not been faithful in their handling of "unrighteous wealth." That is not a reference to multi-millionaires, but to the accumulated money that flows through each of our lives. A person may not feel as if he has much money in his life, but it is worth remembering that a middle-class person making $50,000 a year will have *two million dollars* pass through his hands over a forty-year career. Of course there are bills to be paid, but the choice of standard of living will make a huge difference in determining the amount of resources that are available for Kingdom pursuits. Jesus stated that a person's handling of his money determined whether he could be entrusted with "true riches." This, in my opinion, is not predominantly a reference to more money, but rather to greater spiritual opportunities and responsibilities that have the outcome of a more fruitful ministry and a fuller heart.

Jesus was saying here that *money is a test*. It is not even an advanced test. The two verses taken together presume that being "faithful in the use of unrighteous wealth" is the "faithful in a very little thing" of the previous verse. The way that a Christian spends his money is a *test of his spiritual maturity*.

Allow me to offer a hypothetical example. A church attender has his heart set on living the American Dream and owning as expensive and expansive a home as possible. He buys brand-new premium vehicles that stick him with exorbitant payments each month, but he loves seeing them in the driveway. He "needs" a four-wheeler and a used boat. He does not just spend all he makes; he has substantial credit card debt from the all-too-frequent months when an "emergency" happens and he has no reserve from which to pull. He gives one bill from his wallet every time the offering plate comes by but it usually is one of the smaller denominations. In contrast, the person in the pew behind him has her heart set on seeing as many people as possible meeting Christ and growing spiritually, so she chooses a modest home and drives a used but reliable car. She prayerfully ponders whether a major purchase is truly a want or need. She has to buy shoes for the kids and purchase groceries, but her heart is set on pointing as much of her financial resources as she can toward the Kingdom. Consider these two people: one is passing a spiritual maturity test; one is failing it.

A couple caveats. First, I am fully aware that in some lives greed takes the form of miserly saving rather than the pursuit of a higher standard of living. Certainly there are those in worn clothes living in houses in need of basic repairs who nonetheless are beholden to the god of money within their hearts. In their case, it is the quiet joy they find in that growing balance in the bank that brings their security. This too is a failure of the money test. I am concentrating on the standard of living issue because that is the larger problem in America.

Second, I am aware that the above "American Dream" example does not fully encapsulate the issue here. It is easy to justify the lifestyle that one is living and presume that only those richer are failing this spiritual test. Millard Fuller, founder of Habitat for Humanity, once asked a group of pastors, "Is it possible for a person to build a house so large that it's sinful in the eyes of God? Raise your hand if you think so." There were a couple hundred pastors present and all of them raised their hands. Fuller continued, "Okay, then can you tell me at exactly what size, the precise square footage, a certain house becomes sinful to occupy?" His question was met with silence until finally one pastor in the rear of the room quietly proposed, "When it is bigger than mine."[13] These are matters where each person's situation alters the equation somewhat: the number of kids, income made, the housing market in a given town, the country in which you live, and so on. Each Christian should consider Jesus' teaching and seek to discern the will of the Spirit in her own life when making financial decisions.

Still, the larger truth stands: if American Christians have bought into the American Dream, are passionately pursuing it with abandon and maxed-out credit cards, and are consequently giving minimally to the Kingdom of God, *they are miserably failing a basic spiritual test*. Failing so elementary a test is evidence, in itself, of their spiritual immaturity. This is made worse because they are, when considering either the sweep of human history or even just worldwide incomes today, among the richest people who have ever lived. A solid American middle-class income does not put you in the fiftieth percentile. From either of those larger perspectives, it puts you above the ninety-fifth percentile. Given their current behavior, American Christians as a group face the future of standing before God in judgment as perhaps the group of Christians who collectively wasted the most money on non-Kingdom pursuits.

It Is Not Your Money

My assertions will bother many who are consumed with consumerism and materialism. "It is my money and I have the right to spend it any way I want," they will counter. Well, actually, if you are a follower of Christ, it is not your money.

Jesus immediately followed the "faithful in little" statements with this:

> "And if you have not been faithful in the use of that which is another's, who will give you that which is your own?"[14]

We begin with the first half of the statement. What does "in the use of that which is another's" mean? It means that for a follower of Christ your money does not belong to you.

The idea is simple. Followers of Christ understand that they were "bought with a price" by Jesus.[15] Because of that, they owe everything to Him. One implication of that is when it comes to money they are stewards. A steward is someone who is entrusted to manage the money that belongs to another person. For Christians, their money is not their own, but rather it, like everything else in their lives, belongs to Christ. They are, therefore, stewards of the money flowing through their lives. This is a repeated theme in Jesus' money parables. I will cite just a few examples, beginning with Matthew 25. One of the more familiar lines that preachers use at funerals is:

> "'Well done, good and faithful servant; you were faithful over a few things, I will make you ruler over many things.'"[16]

This line represents the response that the departed Christian desires to hear when Jesus evaluates his faithfulness. What is particularly interesting for this chapter's discussion is that the parable within which this saying is found is one that specifically speaks of *financial* faithfulness. The parable begins with the master distributing funds to three of his servants:

> "Again, the Kingdom of Heaven can be illustrated by the story of a man going on a long trip. He called together his servants and entrusted his money to them while he was gone. He gave five bags of silver to one, two bags of silver to another, and one bag of silver to the last - dividing it in proportion to their abilities. He then left on his trip."[17]

The parable clearly indicates that the master (God) had entrusted financial resources to His servants (Christians). The money was *His* money.

When the master returned, he expected a return on what he had entrusted to each servant:

> "After a long time their master returned from his trip and called them to give an account of how they had used his money. The servant to whom he had entrusted the five bags of silver came forward with five more and said, 'Master, you gave me five bags of silver to invest, and I have earned five more.'"[18]

The master did not give that money to them as a gift; he expected a return on what he had entrusted to them. It is this "return on investment" that earns the "well done" praise from the master. And remember: the praise arose from the correct use of *money*.

Does this mean that God wants us to hoard as much money as possible in this life, put it in the casket when we die, and try to take it to Him? Of course not. Keep in mind the parable of the shrewd servant. We spoke earlier that God wants His people to invest in seeing others come to know Christ and mature along that path. The obvious conclusion here is that Jesus expected His followers to use their money in ways that would bring people to Him. His followers are accountable for how they use His money in this life.

There is a second parable from Jesus that includes the phrase "well done." It appears in Luke 19. The contours of the story are similar: servants are entrusted with substantial funds while their king is away; he then returns and evaluates how the servants did. One notable difference was the return that two of the servants manage:

> "The first servant reported, 'Master, I invested your money and made *ten times the original amount!*' 'Well done!' the king exclaimed."[19]

This servant did not just double the money entrusted to him; he brought about a ten-fold increase. Again, the three points of emphasis are similar for this story: the money was not his; the master expected a return; he was praised for investing well. This parable, though, also touches on an additional point worth mentioning: the follower of Christ who invests His money in the Kingdom can anticipate the power of God multiplying its impact. See, for instance, Jesus' parable of the sower mentioned earlier in this book:

> "But the one who received the seed that fell on good soil is the man who hears the word and understands it. He produces a crop, yielding a hundred, sixty, or thirty times what was sown."[20]

Again, the point is not a "get-rich-quick" scheme, but seeing God's impact flow powerfully through the life of the Christian abandoned to Him. The fruitfulness of that life will be overwhelming.

A third and final parable of Jesus that touches on this theme is in Matthew 21. In this one, a landowner leased his "vineyard to tenant farmers and moved to another country."[21] He then sent various people to "collect his share of the crop," but the tenant farmers refused to listen to his representatives.[22] Eventually, the farmers even killed the landowner's son when he came to collect from them. Jesus then made the point that the Kingdom of God was going to be taken away from the Pharisees and the religious leaders and "given to a people who will produce its fruit."[23] There are a number of worthwhile points here (and some of those were explored earlier in this book's chapter on fruitfulness), but the point to emphasize here is that the landowner expected results from the servants using *what was his.*

In sum, these three parables repeatedly teach that when followers of Christ handle their money they are stewards of funds that actually belong to someone else (God). Christians are sufficiently compromised to their culture that even among those who do tithe few believe that all they have ultimately belongs to God. The Biblical truth on stewardship initially sounds foreign or even un-American. The people of the United States relish their love of the free enterprise system and the economic benefits of capitalism. They know that a fundamental motivation within that system is the opportunity to personally benefit from the work they do and the wealth they create. There is no doubt that capitalism is the most efficient system for making wealth, although Christians rarely acknowledge the selfish motivation of personal greed that spurs that efficiency.

The Biblical idea of stewardship places followers of Christ in a different place than the default position within capitalism. Stewardship, as evidenced in the three above passages, teaches that because a person belongs to Christ, the money that comes into her life is not her own. It ultimately belongs to Christ. Because of that, she is accountable to use it in ways that are pleasing to *Him*. Part of Final Judgment will include a person's faithfulness and fruitfulness in her use of her money.

Properly understood and incorporated into American Christians' financial lives, Biblical stewardship would serve as a powerful antidote to the materialism and consumerism of American culture. It would help Christians to understand that perpetually raising their standard of living is not supposed to be their monetary goal. It would help Christians to focus their spending on ways that would, whenever possible, draw people to Christ. It would help Christians in their ongoing efforts to discern between wants and needs.

Of course, as Christians presently live, this almost never happens. To take one commonly cited example, the percentage of Christians who tithe to their church is abysmal, usually registering around one in ten.[24] That is pathetic, but in line with a group of people spending their resources on the American Dream instead of the Kingdom of God. (And this does not even consider the idea that many American Christians could and should be giving substantially more than ten percent.) In fact, "Christians give less today per capita than during the Great Depression."[25] Back then the mean per capita giving was 3.3 percent while today it is only 2.5 percent.[26]

To cite another example, by all outward appearances Christians appear as enthralled by the financial aspects of the pursuit of the American Dream as the rest of the culture. The standard of living of Christians and non-Christians of similar income show no substantial disparity in the vast majority of cases. Of all the issues on which Christians take a strong stand (i.e. abortion, homosexuality, etc.), money and greed are completely missing from that list. Christians are not known to have any critique of the pursuit of wealth and possessions as a sound life goal.

Returning to this section's starting verse, the second half of Luke 16:12 is more challenging: "who will give you that which is your own?" Given the previous verse's comment about "true riches" that are not financial in nature, it seems likely that Jesus has something similar in mind here. If Christians are unwilling to be faithful stewards of wealth that belongs to their Lord, they have cut themselves off from greater opportunities and authority within Christ's Kingdom.

The God of America

We have almost made it to the verse in Luke 16 where it speaks of the Pharisees as "lovers of money." Before we get there, though, there is one more verse from Jesus – and it may be the toughest of all. Jesus boldly declared:

> "No servant can serve two masters; for either he will hate the one and love the other, or else he will be devoted to the one and despise the other. You cannot serve God and wealth."[27]

The god of America is money. Allow me to repeat myself: the god of America is money. This, to my mind, is beyond dispute. The American Dream is largely financial in nature. One of our main goals for our children is that they will have a better life than we do – and when we say that, we are thinking "financially better." We love and applaud those who make millions. We have countless shows and books that celebrate the wealthy lifestyle. The amount of debt we have amassed in the pursuit of the American Dream is truly mind-boggling.

While Americans heartily debate issues like abortion and homosexuality, there is surprisingly little discussion of monetary sins. That we should live as we do concerning our finances is simply a given in our society. The greatest sins in a society are rarely the ones that are actively debated; they are almost always the ones that are completely accepted as normal by the population at large. For America, that concerns money. Even within the church, aside from the occasional pastoral request for tithing, there is shamefully little sermon discussion of the intrinsic dangers of money. Given America's materialistic obsessions and Jesus' statement that a person cannot serve both God and money, one would presume that wealth and possessions would be a major and regular subject from the pulpit. It is not – and that is further proof that love of money is America's greatest sin.

Given such a materialistic culture, what an opportunity is present for Christians to stand out by obeying the teaching of Christ on money! What an open door there is to point to eternal things by gently but firmly refusing to capitulate to a life of endlessly pursuing more stuff. Instead, Christians have crumpled under the pressure of capitalistic pursuits and bought wholeheartedly into the American Dream.

Given that massive failure, Jesus' words become frightening in the extreme. He says that you *cannot* serve two masters. A life devoted to money, possessions, and wealth will, by its very nature, preclude a person from being the follower of Christ that he needs to be. A life devoted to money pushes the one true God off the throne of a person's life. American Christians show every outward sign of having done exactly that.

Scoffing at Him

This leads to the climax of this section, which includes this chapter's title. After Jesus shared all this money teaching, we read the reaction it got from the Pharisees:

> Now the Pharisees, who were *lovers of money*, were listening to all these things and were *scoffing at Him*.[28]

The "all these things" refers to the teaching that this chapter has reviewed up to this point: the parable of the shrewd manager that taught to use what you control to accomplish your goal; the expectation that Christ's followers would be faithful in the test of their "use of unrighteous wealth" so that He could entrust greater responsibilities to them; the stewardship of the money that passed through their lives, with that money actually belonging to Christ; the impossibility of serving both God and wealth. To all this, the Pharisees' response to Christ was disbelief.

I imagine there is a fair amount of scoffing among the American Christians reading this book at the truths I have shared so far from Luke 16. For some, the scoffing will be that I must be a liberal lunatic to have the audacity to even marginally question anything capitalistic. For some, the scoffing will be that I am arguing that financial things have direct relevance to their spiritual lives when they are confident money matters should be carefully compartmentalized away from their faith life. For some, the scoffing will be that Jesus actually expects a lower standard of living, with the reader driving older cars and living in a smaller home than at present. For some, while they agree with my points, the scoffing will be that Jesus would actually expect them to rearrange such substantial parts of their lives.

At its base, the reasons for all these various forms of scoffing have the same genesis as the Pharisees on this issue: the love of money. American Christians love money. They are sold out to the capitalistic system. They have bought into the American Dream. They are pursuing upward mobility. There is scant evidence to the contrary. American Christians look just like the rest of American culture on this issue. To reach that point, they have ignored a host of Bible passages that are, for them, apparently hiding in plain sight.

Hiding in Plain Sight

It is almost beyond explanation how American Christians can simultaneously claim to be people of the Word and yet be so myopic in their approach to money. The Biblical references to money, greed, and wealth are frequent, obvious, and unequivocal. Still, American Christians somehow not only fail to pursue those teachings, but actually have convinced themselves that the passionate pursuit of all for which the American Dream stands is a patriotic and religious duty.

Christians love to find comfort during the trials of life from God's promise that "Never will I leave you; never will I forsake you."[29] Yet the actual context of the promise in Hebrews 13 is financial:

> Keep your lives free from the love of money and be content with what you have, because God has said, "Never will I leave you; never will I forsake you."[30]

Christians quote the latter part as a vague spiritual assurance they may claim for their hearts. They do this while divorcing it from the former part, which would bring practical financial changes in their lives.

Why do Christians ignore Paul's advice to Timothy?

> But godliness with contentment is great gain. For we brought nothing into the world, and we can take nothing out of it.[31]

That does not sound like advice to take to the mall. Paul continued:

> Those who want to get rich fall into temptation and a trap and into many foolish and harmful desires that plunge people into ruin and destruction.[32]

Rather than embracing the pursuit of material wealth, Paul seemed to have an alternate take: there is great spiritual danger in the pursuit of wealth and possessions. He pressed his case:

> For the love of money is a root of all kinds of evil. Some people, eager for money, have wandered from the faith and pierced themselves with many griefs.[33]

He does not sound as if he got the capitalist memo.

Jesus was especially pointed in Luke 6:

> "But woe to you who are rich, for you have already received your comfort. Woe to you who are well fed now, for you will go hungry."[34]

That has to mean something other than it initially appears or American Christians have completely missed Jesus' heart on wealth.

There are many more verses worth sharing, but for the sake of brevity I will close. In Luke 12 Jesus told the story of a wealthy man who found his business so successful that he had to build bigger storage facilities to handle it all. He rejoiced in how great his life was.[35] He was, in brief, the epitome of the American Dream. The story ends with God speaking to the man:

> "But God said to him, 'You fool! This very night your life will be demanded from you. Then who will get what you have prepared for yourself?'"[36]

It sounds very much as if God is emphatically rejecting the American Dream. Jesus hammered this home with His conclusion to the parable:

> "This is how it will be with whoever stores up things for themselves but is not rich toward God."[37]

As if that was not clear enough, this parable was told right after Jesus instructed someone:

> "Be on your guard against all kinds of greed; life does not consist in the abundance of possessions."[38]

These are abundantly clear and give a vision of a financial life at odds with business as usual for America. Americans are unrepentant in their passion and pursuit of material gain. Americans are lovers of money. On this issue, it is clear that American Christians are better Americans than Christians.

Chapter Ten

"Woe to You, You Hypocrites!"

Scorched earth, dirty dishes, and whitewashed tombs

For many people, the single word that best characterizes modern American Christians is "hypocrites." It is a painful charge, but one that has clung to us for some time now. It was also an accusation that Jesus repeatedly threw at the Pharisees.

Once, before a crowd of "many thousands," Jesus taught:

> "Be on your guard against the yeast of
> the Pharisees, which is *hypocrisy*."[1]

This warning against the "yeast of the Pharisees" was repeated multiple places in the gospels.[2] In one passage, the "yeast" is defined as "the teaching of the Pharisees and Sadducees."[3] What does this mean? Hypocrisy is pretending to be one thing when you actually are something else. In its most common use, yeast is something put into bread to make it rise. It "puffs up" the dough. The Pharisees' teaching looked substantial to the casual observer, but led to a hypocritical religion rather than genuine closeness to God.

In the gospels, there are several practical examples of exactly how Jesus thought the Pharisees' approach was hypocritical. Jesus thought their giving to the Temple was rife with hypocrisy:

> "So when you give to the needy, do
> not announce it with trumpets, as the
> *hypocrites* do in the synagogues and on
> the streets, to be honored by men. I

tell you the truth, they have received their reward in full."[4]

Why was this an act of hypocrisy? Because they claimed to be giving to honor God, but what they were really after was the attention and praise of people. Thus they announced their giving with trumpets out where everyone would see. Jesus said "they have received their reward in full." The reward they actually wanted was the public attention and Jesus confirmed that was the only reward they would see. God would not reward them eternally for giving done hypocritically.

A similar example followed concerning prayer:

> "And when you pray, do not be like the *hypocrites*, for they love to pray standing in the synagogues and on the street corners to be seen by men. I tell you the truth, they have received their reward in full."[5]

It was the same thing here. Prayer is supposed to be personal communication between someone and God. These folks, though, had turned it into a performance, "speaking to God" out where they were assured their prayers would also be heard by the crowd. They too had "received their reward in full," meaning they had received their public praise and should not expect to hear from God anytime soon.

Jesus also found hypocrisy in how people judged others. He taught:

> "Why do you look at the speck of sawdust in your brother's eye and pay no attention to the plank in your own eye? How can you say to your brother, 'Let me take the speck out of your eye,' when all the time there is a plank in your own eye? You *hypocrite*, first take the plank out of your own eye, and then you will see clearly to

remove the speck from your brother's eye."⁶

These people were quick to point out the problems in others' lives while simultaneously ignoring the sin in their own life. If you hate sin, you should hate it wherever you see it – in your life or in someone else's life. To act as if you have it all together while condemning someone else's shortcomings is simply hypocritical.

An Entire Chapter Trashing the Pharisees

Matthew 23 stands as the high point (low point?) of Jesus' condemnation of the Pharisees. The entire chapter is a lengthy, scorching sermon against their sins. We handled the first twelve verses in the chapter "Whoever Exalts Himself Shall Be Humbled." Now we turn our attention to the "woe" portion of the chapter. Over and over, Jesus condemned the Pharisees with the phrase "Woe to you, teachers of the law and Pharisees"⁷ (or some variant of that). Some people who have never actually read the Bible have a picture of Jesus as a Mr. Rogers figure, who only spoke words of comfort and encouragement. This chapter is one that completely destroys that notion. Jesus was pointed, harsh, and relentless in His criticism.

In a similar passage in Luke 11, Jesus shared this type of "woe" accusations toward the Pharisees. One of the "experts in the law" complained to Jesus, saying, "Teacher, when [You] say these things, [You] insult us also."⁸ It is obvious that he presumed Jesus was unaware of how harsh His words were coming across and that He would apologize. Instead, Jesus responded, "And you experts in the law, woe to you"⁹ and then lit them up with three criticisms of their behavior. It is clear that Jesus did not wear a cardigan.

I want to spend the remainder of this chapter looking at the specifics of the accusations that Jesus made toward the Pharisees in Matthew 23. What were the ways that Jesus found the Pharisees to be hypocritical? Just as important, do Christians share those characteristics?

Hypocritical on Evangelism

The first two "woes" concern evangelism. The first is in verse 13:

> "Woe to you, teachers of the law and Pharisees, you *hypocrites*! You shut the kingdom of heaven in men's faces. You yourselves do not enter, nor will you let those enter who are trying to."[10]

Why would people who said they loved God deliberately keep people away from Him? What was at issue here was not a person saying he wanted to know God and the Pharisee responding, "Nope, you are not allowed to try to get near Him." The Pharisees undoubtedly believed that they were helping as many people as possible get to God. The problem was that did not actually happen.

Think of the person who begins to recognize the need for God in her life. Perhaps she endures the death of someone dear to her and begins to think about life beyond this life. Perhaps she is burdened by guilt and is hopeful that divine forgiveness is possible. Whatever the specific situation, she begins to take steps in the direction of God.

To whom would she turn? Obviously, the religious experts would be the place to start. In Jesus' day, it would likely have been the Pharisees. As she looked to the Pharisees, one of two thoughts would probably come to mind. One was that they were hypocrites. They talked about all this God stuff, but they did not seem godlier. Second, she would consider what the Pharisees said you had to do to get close to God and likely think to herself, "That is impossible." Earlier in Matthew 23, Jesus accused the Pharisees of being quick to "tie up heavy loads and put them on men's shoulders, but they themselves are not willing to lift a finger to move them."[11] He was speaking of spiritual burdens – demanding that the people follow a list of rules that was impossible to faithfully complete.

Here is the point: in either case, the person who was interested in getting closer to God found the Pharisee standing beside the door saying, "You know what you have to do if you want to walk through this door?" and then laying out a burdensome list. The person ready to walk through the door toward God instead walked away discouraged.

More to the point of this hypocrisy chapter: sometimes the reason that a person showing some interest in God did not walk through that door was the hypocrisy of the "true believers." In Jesus' day, the person perhaps had those heart longings, but then looked at the Pharisees and thought, "If I have to be like that to get to God, no thanks."

Are Christians guilty of this? Without question. In more than twenty years as a pastor, I can tell you that the number of people who are unwilling to "come to Christ" because of intellectual or theological concerns are pretty limited. The number of people is vast who are unwilling because of the hypocrisy they have seen in Christians. To share a widely known statement from Brennan Manning:

> The greatest single cause of atheism in the world today is Christians who acknowledge Jesus with their lips and walk out the door and deny Him by their lifestyle. That is what an unbelieving world simply finds unbelievable.[12]

With church being the "default option" on getting to God in much of the United States, how many people have felt longings to walk in the direction of God, but then stopped because of Christian hypocrisy? If becoming an Christian is the only way to walk through that door, then they would rather stay on the outside looking in.

The second church that I had the privilege to pastor was a new church start. We were starting from nothing – no people, no building, and no money. Our focus was to be a church for people who had given up on church. As I began sharing the vision publicly, I thought that I would get a substantial amount of flak from Christians who were already in existing traditional churches. Things like, "What's wrong with the churches we have now?" or "Don't we have enough churches already?" In the many conversations I had with Christians about the church start, I had exactly two accusatory conversations like that. Instead, what I heard countless times from Christians broke my heart. "You know, my granddaughter used to go to church, but . . . ." "My son grew up in church, but . . . ." "My husband will occasionally go to church with me, but . . . ." The stories varied, but all had a common theme: the hypocrisy of Christians. The granddaughter who would not go back to church because of the hypocrisy she had seen in the life of her youth group leader. The son taken to church since he was on the cradle roll, but no longer able to stomach the blatant duplicity of the lives of so many church members. The husband who knew too much about too many Sunday morning attendees and wanted no more than a passing association with those people. These conversations kept returning to people who had been driven away from church or who refused to start church because of what they had seen in the lives of those attending church. *And these were Christians sharing these stories.*

The bottom line is this: there are countless people with interest in drawing closer to God who have been kept from entering through that door because they see Christians standing beside it. Jesus called the Pharisees hypocrites and said,

> "You yourselves will not enter, nor will you let those enter who are trying to."[13]

Christians are often doing exactly this to the "seekers" who are interested in God but repelled by Christian hypocrisy.

We now move on to the related verse that follows verse 13:

> "Woe to you, teachers of the law and Pharisees, you *hypocrites*! You travel over land and sea to win a single convert, and when he becomes one, you make him twice as much a son of hell as you are."[14]

Our previous discussion explained why so many are repelled by Christians rather than drawn to God through them. What about those who *do* walk through the door? What about those who *do* convert to the Christian understanding of God?

This is a point of great joy in conservative Christian circles – seeing someone "get saved." Evangelicals are an evangelistic people. They believe it is essential for believers to "share their faith." That is, to witness to people about Jesus in the hope that they will "invite Christ into their hearts." The go-to passage for this is the "Great Commission" from Jesus at the end of Matthew:

> "All authority has been given to Me in heaven and on earth. Go therefore and make disciples of all the nations, baptizing them in the name of the Father and the Son and the Holy Spirit."[15]

This fervor for souls is considered one of the most unassailable proofs that conservative Christians are God's people. How could they be so passionate for people to come to know God if they are not the true representatives of His name? The deeply troubling aspect of the Matthew 23 verse I just shared is that it points out that *the Pharisees were evangelistic*.

The Matthew 23 verse tells us Pharisees made significant sacrifices ("travel over land and sea") even if it only resulted in one soul coming to God. Does this remind anyone else of the missionary focus that Christians have? They have sent missionaries around the globe in an effort to "win the world" to Jesus. Again, this "heart for missions" is seen as indisputable evidence of a true faith.

To be clear, the problem is not the evangelistic fervor. The problem is the result: after going to all that trouble to win someone to Jesus, they then "disciple him" so that he can become just like them. In fact, the new convert may be even more passionate about all this than his mentors, making him "twice as much a son of hell as you are." The longer-established believer might have settled down or become compromised on some issues, but the sold-out new believer may well want to passionately follow every teaching that he can find.

In the end, evangelism is only a good thing if a person is converted to be an actual follower of God. If he instead becomes a follower of a group of hypocrites, he has just become a converted "son of hell." If Christians can point to their passion for evangelism but cannot point to large number of converts who are actually

Christlike, they are in the exact place Jesus accused the Pharisees of standing.

Misplaced Focus

Moving forward, the next two "woes" are also related to each other. Both have to do with focusing on the wrong things within faith. Verses 16-22 have to do with focusing on the wrong thing within a given issue; verses 23-24 have to do with focusing on the wrong issues within faith life.

The "woe" in verse 16 is the only one within this larger passage that does not include a direct reference to "hypocrites," instead referring to the Pharisees as "blind guides." We will include it in our discussion because of its place within the larger passage. Jesus proclaimed:

> "Woe to you, blind guides! You say, 'If anyone swears by the temple, it means nothing; but if anyone swears by the gold of the temple, he is bound by his oath.' You blind fools! Which is greater: the gold, or the temple that makes the gold sacred? You also say, 'If anyone swears by the altar, it means nothing; but if anyone swears by the gift on it, he is bound by his oath.' You blind men! Which is greater: the gift, or the altar that makes the gift sacred? Therefore, he who swears by the altar swears by it and everything on it. And he who swears by the temple swears by it and by the one who dwells in it. And he who swears by heaven swears by God's throne and by the one who sits on it."[16]

The origins of these particular distinctions (gold versus temple, gift versus altar) are unknown, but their outline is clear. Here we have an issue of honesty – that is, keeping your promises or vows. The Pharisees made ridiculous rules on this. If you swore by the temple, you were not obligated to keep your promise; if, however, you swore by the gold of the temple, then you had to keep your vow. If you swore by the altar, you were not obligated to keep your promise; if, however, you swore by the gift on the altar, then you had to keep your vow. It all flew in the face of Jesus' simple instruction on vows in the Sermon on the Mount:

> "Simply let your 'Yes' be 'Yes,' and your 'No,' 'No'; anything beyond this comes from the evil one."[17]

Rather than simply being honest people who meant what they said, the Pharisees developed rules that allowed them some wiggle room to accomplish what they wanted.

The larger point of Jesus' words in this section of Matthew 23 was not directly about honesty and vows; it was about *focusing on the wrong thing within a given issue*. Here, the issue was vows. They focused on when they had to actually keep their promises rather than focusing on being people of integrity in all they said. Many times religious folks rightly declare something an important matter but then proceed to give their attention to the wrong aspect of that issue.

Do Christians do this? Do they focus on the wrong point within a given issue? Yes, frequently. I will limit myself to five examples of Christians doing this very thing. Several of these issues are ripe for extensive discussions, but I will be brief.

1. The war on Christmas.

A favorite annual whipping post for conservative Christians is the "war on Christmas." Every holiday season in recent years a collection of stories has been gathered about companies who refuse to allow their employees to say, "Merry Christmas" to customers or towns that change their "Christmas Parade" into a "Holiday Parade." Such things are deemed to be a horrible assault on the sanctity of the day of Christ's birth. This is also trumpeted as proof of the declining influence of Christians in America and the rise of godless liberalism.

There may well be a substantive issue surrounding Christmas, but it is not the one about which Christians endlessly fuss. In America, the birth of Christ has been transformed into a consumeristic orgy. It is by far the biggest sales season of the year for retailers, who relentlessly push the need for people to buy, buy, buy. Recent years have seen the introduction of sales on Thanksgiving Day, which used to be off-limits. Apparently it is now too much to ask to have one day a year to not buy anything but just be thankful for the blessings we already have.

The larger point regarding Christmas is this: is the problem that the greeter at Walmart or the local mall says "Happy Holidays" instead of "Merry Christmas" as I come to shop, or is the problem that I spend so much of my Christmas season pursuing materialistic acquisition in the first place? Is the problem how they greet me at Walmart or the mall, or that I am at those places so much? Jesus said,

> "Foxes have dens and birds have nests, but the Son of Man has no place to lay his head."[18]

Jesus owned almost nothing, had no home, and we have turned His birthday into the biggest buying spree of the year? And as that is happening, Christians are complaining about how they are greeted at the store's door? Are they focused on the wrong point within this issue?

2. Sanctity of marriage.

Conservative Christians have loudly and frequently decried the legalization of homosexual marriage. In recent years, it has surpassed abortion as the main political focal point of evangelical fury. In arguing against homosexual marriage, a frequently repeated statement is that it destroys the "sanctity of marriage." Conservative Christians proudly proclaim that they want to do all they can to preserve the sanctity of marriage.

Conservative Christians have been vehement in their opposition to homosexual marriage. Even given such passion, the practical reality is there is relatively little that they can do regarding the legalization of homosexual marriage. They can vote for representatives politically who will espouse their views, but those opportunities are infrequent and second-hand.

There is, however, one much more direct thing they could do to preserve the sanctity of marriage: fewer heterosexual divorces within the church. In that regard, their opportunities would be frequent and first-hand. There are relatively few homosexuals in most conservative Christian churches, but there are a lot of married heterosexuals. Those married heterosexuals obviously have great daily opportunity to make their own marriages examples of the sanctity of marriage. A people who truly cherish the sanctity of marriage would obviously pursue this.

Allow me to be clear: my argument here is not meant to condemn conservative Christians who have had to divorce because of Biblically allowable reasons. I understand the heartache and pain; as a pastor, I have counseled many people through that dark valley. My argument rather is focused on conservative Christian leaders. To loudly decry homosexual marriage as destructive to the sanctity of marriage when they have relatively little influence on that issue while simultaneously remaining abjectly silent on the issue of heterosexual divorce is straightforward hypocrisy. If they really cared about the sanctity of marriage, they would work for its preservation on all fronts, *especially the ones where they have great influence*. But they do not. Most conservative Christian pastors have not preached a sermon on the Bible's teaching about divorce, because they know what a sensitive subject it is and they are worried about making their tithers mad. Instead, they spew rhetoric concerning the part of the sanctity of marriage issue where they have little influence (but where there is little pushback from within their church). Are they focused on the wrong point within this issue?

3. Worship.

The last thirty years in the American church has seen the lingering conflict known as "worship wars." On the one hand are those who love contemporary music, who want a full band, and who prefer lots of praise choruses; on the other, those who enjoy hymns, who like piano and organ, and want traditional music. Many angry business meetings have taken place in churches over transitioning the worship from traditional to contemporary. Many churches have split over this issue. The arguing has seemed to be endless.

What is interesting within this whole debate, now decades old, is that the focus is on what the *person* prefers. "I get a lot out of the old hymns." "Praise choruses speak to my heart." The focus has been on form. Lost within that is the fundamental truth that worship is ultimately not supposed to be about pleasing us, but about pleasing God. Is it possible that God has been looking on both groups and thinking, "I am not a big fan of either of you all because you are both focused on the wrong thing"? Could it be the lack of a sense of the Spirit in so many services, whether it is because the service feels musty and old or because it feels like a rock concert, is because few have been focused on the larger issue of pleasing God in worship? Instead Christians in both camps on this issue too often presume they are the ultimate audience for the music. Are they focused on the wrong point within this issue?

4. **Spiritual maturity.**

In most conservative Christian churches, those who are deemed to be "the faithful" are usually those who show up for all three services each week – Sunday morning, Sunday evening, and Wednesday evening. These are considered to be the "pillars of the church." Of course, the problem with that is that showing up three times a week to "sit and soak" is not necessarily a sign of spiritual maturity as much as regularity.

What about depth of compassion? What about Christlikeness? What about prayer life? There are lots of better ways to evaluate spiritual maturity. Yet within churches people will lament those who seem to be spiritually growing but still do not bother to show up for additional services. The presumption is that something must be awry for anyone wanting to be spiritually mature to not show up to services as much as possible. Are they focused on the wrong point within this issue?

5. **Prayer in schools.**

One persistent thorn in conservative Christians' side is the long-standing prohibition on prayer in schools. It is one of the "greatest hits" many evangelical pastors pull out when detailing the slide of America from a "Christian nation" into "godless liberalism." The presumption often is that God would greatly bless our nation again if prayer was again allowed in public schools.

There is a related question worth considering: how many Christian families with kids at home pray together each day? The answer is not encouraging. Is it not odd for Christians to want to defer daily prayer for their children onto a secular school system when absolutely nothing prohibits them from praying together as a family? Should the parents not be the ones taking the lead here and not the public school teachers? And if Christian parents did take the lead, would that not do an even better job of doing what Christians say they want: kids getting to pray? Are they focused on the wrong point within this issue?

In all these examples, we find that Christians are doing the same type of things that the Pharisees were: focusing on the wrong point within a given issue.

Now we turn to verses 23-24 and the Pharisees' focus on the wrong matters with faith life. Jesus continued His "woes":

> "Woe to you, teachers of the law and Pharisees, you hypocrites! You give a tenth of your spices – mint, dill and cumin. But you have neglected the more important matters of the law – justice, mercy and faithfulness. You should have practiced the latter, without neglecting the former. You blind guides! You strain out a gnat but swallow a camel."[19]

Here Jesus accused the Pharisees of prioritizing the wrong matters in their religion. They were faithful to tithe even the most obscure of their acquisitions – the spices that they grew. I am sure they thought precision in such a minor matter was evidence of their insider status. The problem was that, while they were attending to such trivialities, they were neglecting the more important matters, like justice, mercy, and faithfulness. Jesus then concluded His point with the memorable image of straining out a gnat but swallowing a camel. Both of those were unclean animals according to the Mosaic Law.[20] The Pharisees would sometimes literally strain their drinks just to be certain they were not accidently swallowing a gnat and inadvertently breaking the Law. While being meticulous in that tiny matter, though, they were blatantly ignoring many of the more essential portions of the Law (and, thus, metaphorically, swallowing a camel).

Do Christians do similar things? I will look in turn at these "more important matters" that Jesus mentions: justice, mercy, and faithfulness.

1. Justice.

"Justice issues" are often seen by conservative Christians as the prerogative of mainline Christians. The problem may be that the topics do not fit into the normal conservative political issues matrix through which many conservative Christians see the world. The problem may be that the issues do not personally benefit a typical conservative Christian. Whatever the reason, "justice" is generally not a high priority for conservative Christians.

Here is an example: the long-term struggles of the black community in America. Much has been written on the problem, but I will limit myself to a summary statement:

> Blacks are more than 2.5 times as likely to live in poverty as whites. Unemployment among African Americans is more than twice as high; more than a quarter of black households are food insecure (compared to 11 percent of white households); and during the Great Recession, African Americans were three times as likely to have their

200

utilities cut off and face foreclosure or eviction.[21]

This is a substantial justice issue with far-reaching implications. It is a systemic problem that is decades old and shows few signs of improvement. And conservative Christians *do not care*. Their leadership rarely addresses the issue – they are too consumed with other priorities. I understand that this is a complex issue and multitude of factors must be considered, including some self-destructive patterns of behavior within the black community. My point is simply that there is the appearance of a serious injustice and conservative Christians have responded with a shrug of the shoulders.

If Jesus was concerned about the poor and marginalized, why would Christians not be vocal in pursuing justice on this issue? Is it because "justice issues" are not for them, despite what Jesus said in Matthew 23:23? Is it because they have little personal stake in this injustice? Is it because the issue does not fit the Republican political platform and therefore is not a political priority for many Christians? Is it because the conservative Christian church in America is overwhelmingly white? I will not pretend to have a comprehensive answer to this issue, but two things I can say with certainty: this is a justice issue and conservative Christians do not care about it.

2. Mercy.

The second "more important matter of the law" that Jesus mentioned was mercy. Now grace and mercy are two things of which Christians often speak in the context of salvation. "Today is the day to grab onto the mercy of God and be saved!" When it comes to mercy in just about any other context, though, Christians do not fare as well.

As an example, consider the issue of foster children. There are more than 400,000 children in the foster care system in the United States.[22] In most of their situations, they are in need of a loving family to foster them through their biological family's time of struggle. There are approximately 300,000 churches in America.[23] The answer seems pretty obvious, does it not: if only one family in each church in America stepped up to show mercy to these kids in dire need, most of the need for foster families would be filled. Only it's not.

A small amount of credit does need to be given here to the church leaders who have tried to raise the profile of this issue as part of their commitment to being pro-life. There are not many of them, but there are a few. One wonders why this is not a burden on more church leaders when you consider James 1:27:

> Religion that God our Father accepts as pure and faultless is this: to *look after orphans* and widows in their distress and to keep oneself from being polluted by the world.[24]

Foster kids are "temporary orphans," as they need someone to care for them in their time of crisis.

There have been few church leaders who have been outspoken on this issue, but more to the point, there have been few Christians who have been willing to step up with a heart of *mercy*. Here we are in what many Christians love to (erroneously) proclaim a "Christian nation" with hundreds of thousands of vulnerable children in need of mercy and few Christians stepping up to provide it.

A thought experiment: what if Christians were as vocal and vehement about finding a home for every foster child in America as they are in denouncing homosexual marriage? What if pastors frequently found themselves slipping references to this problem into their sermons as they preached from their heart's passion? What if this was an issue that church laity could not get off their mind? Further, what would such an occurrence do to the reputation of the church to the unbelieving world around them?

3. Faithfulness.

The third "more important matter" that Jesus mentioned was "faithfulness." That is the English word that the New International Version uses here for the translation of the Greek word "pistis," although modern translations are split on whether to translate it as "faith" or "faithfulness."[25] I hold that both are included here: believing in the right things (faith) and holding to those beliefs even when they become costly (faithfulness).

A couple of examples on this point. First, prayer. Christians are quick to proclaim the necessity of prayer. They include prayer in their worship services and usually open and close their meetings with prayer. Yet the actual private prayer faithfulness of Christians is spotty at best. As a pastor for over twenty years, I can tell you that the number of strong prayer lives within most churches is pretty limited. Prayer is something Christians say is crucial, but then fail to actually bathe their lives in that.

Second, struggling people. Jesus obviously spent a disproportionate amount of His time with those who had substantial problems. The default desire in churches is for the congregation to grow, but that those newcomers who bring the growth be "church broken."[26] That is, they know the right way to act in church, know the behaviors that are deemed off-limits, and fit in well with the existing congregation. It is a recurring story: the new person (maybe a recently hired youth pastor or a family member who gets saved) begins successfully inviting the "wrong people" to an established congregation. What ensues is not an open embrace of those whose lives are a mess; rather, in almost every telling, it is a defense of the church's comfortable status quo. One would presume that churches would want the struggling, the hurting, the broken, the hopeless. In truth, most do not. They are too disruptive to the established order.

In sum, these two Matthew 23 "woes" also fit Christians too well, with many examples that can be easily applied. Both "woes" have to do with focusing on the wrong points within their faith. Verses 16-22 have to do with focusing on the wrong matter within a given issue; verses 23-24 have to do with focusing on the wrong issues within faith life. Christians are guilty on both counts.

Dirty Dishes

Now we have a third pair of "woes," with these relating to the type of righteousness that the Pharisees possessed. Matthew 23:25-26 looks at who the Pharisees were and then verses 27-28 consider who they appeared to be to those around them. In neither case do they come out very well.

First we have verses 25-26:

> "Woe to you, teachers of the law and Pharisees, you *hypocrites*! You clean the outside of the cup and dish, but inside they are full of greed and self-indulgence. Blind Pharisee! First clean the inside of the cup and dish, and then the outside also will be clean."[27]

Part of the Pharisees' meticulous keeping of their rules was ceremonial washing. As the Bible shares in Mark 7:

> The Pharisees and all the Jews do not eat unless they give their hands a ceremonial washing, holding to the tradition of the elders. When they come from the marketplace they do not eat unless they wash. And they observe many other traditions, such as the washing of cups, pitchers and kettles.[28]

It was to this that Jesus alluded when He said that the Pharisees "clean the outside of the cup and dish," but then contrasted that legalistic nicety with what was actually within their hearts – "greed and self-indulgence." The picture is clear: the Pharisees had their outward rules to make them pure, but those rules did not impact who they truly were within their hearts. Jesus then gave the principle they should have known: if you clean the inside first, then the outside will be clean too. If a believer takes care of the inward matters of spirituality, the outward aspects will take care of themselves.

Is this a picture of Christians? I have shared at various points in this book the simple, tragic fact: Christians are not Christlike. They are not consistently obedient to the teaching of Christ. They have a form of religion, but not one that leads to a transformed life. That, sadly, puts them square in the bulls-eye of Jesus' words here: who they are inside is not who Christ intends them to be.

Jesus then shared a related "woe":

> "Woe to you, teachers of the law and Pharisees, you *hypocrites*! You are like whitewashed tombs, which look beautiful on the outside but inside are full of dead men's bones and everything unclean. In the same way, on the outside you appear to people as righteous but on the inside you are full of *hypocrisy* and wickedness."[29]

The Pharisees looked religious, but it was a deceptive picture. Back in Jesus' day, many towns whitewashed tombs. This had the ritual benefit of helping people to know where bodies were so that they would not accidentally make contact with the grave site and become "unclean." It also had a beautification effect – a fresh coat of paint makes most things look better. Jesus compared the Pharisees to those whitewashed tombs. The grave sites looked nice outwardly, but were nasty on the inside. So too were the Pharisees.

Is this a picture of Christians? Again, this is a point we have repeatedly come to throughout the book. Christians look religious, but their lives are not changed. It is the very reason that today there is such disunity between what people think of the church and what they think of Jesus. Many non-believers are fans of Jesus; few are fans of the church. If the church is supposed to be filled with people who look and live like Jesus, why the disparity? Sure, churches are beautiful architecturally and believers clean up nicely on Sunday morning – all giving the outward appearance of righteousness, but it is what is inside that matters.

Not Like Them

This brings us to the last "woe," which concerned the Pharisees continuing what their forefathers did:

> "Woe to you, teachers of the law and Pharisees, you *hypocrites*! You build tombs for the prophets and decorate the graves of the righteous. And you say, 'If we had lived in the days of our forefathers, we would not have taken part with them in shedding the blood of the prophets.' So you testify against yourselves that you are the descendants of those who murdered the prophets. Fill up, then, the measure of the sin of your forefathers!"[30]

The fundamental issue here dwelt in the Old Testament history of Israel refusing to hear God's word of rebuke. It was an oft-repeated pattern: Israel drifted away from God, God sent a prophet to point them back to Him, but the man of God got mocked, imprisoned, or even killed for the divine message he shared. The Pharisees looked back on those times and declared that if they had been around they certainly would not have joined Israel in its disobedience. Jesus condemned them, though, acknowledging that they were verbally admitting to being the children of those "descendents . . . who murdered the prophets" while their hypocritical lives gave no reason to believe that they would have actually stood for what God wanted in those moments. They were claiming to be the true people of God while simultaneously acknowledging that their ancestors were the enemies of God. In such a situation, you obviously need considerable proof to show that the present group is different than their forefathers. That proof was completely lacking.

Are Christians in the same situation? This entire book has been pressing that case. The primary argument this book has made is that Christians share many of the characteristics of the Pharisees and that is evidence Christians are wildly off-course. Jesus' argument fits perfectly here: "You Christians claim that if you had lived back in gospel times that you would have stood up for Me and condemned the Pharisees. And yet you do the very things in your religious lives today that they did two thousand years ago. You are cut from the same cloth as them; you live your religious lives in a way that evokes their characteristics and priorities. You are not the good guys in this story; you are the bad guys. You are not the people of God; you are the enemies of Jesus."

Conclusion

Matthew 23 is a scorched earth chapter. Jesus leaves little in His wake. It is easy to see how the Pharisees would be enraged against Christ after such confrontation.

I shared earlier that "hypocrite" is one of the words the American public most associates with Christians. This chapter, I believe, proves that their perception is correct. It is easy to minimize hypocrisy under the guise of "well, no one is perfect – of course we are all a little bit hypocritical." That is not what we are talking about here. I am not arguing that Christians are imperfect but at least they are pretty close. I am arguing that too often we are pretenders. I am arguing that our internal spiritual life is frequently nothing like what God desires. I am arguing that we have an outward form of righteousness, but not one that actually gets us closer to God. I am arguing that often we are hypocrites, worthy of the same horrible fury that Jesus unleashed on the Pharisees in Matthew 23.

Perhaps I am wrong and Christians should happily continue to do what they have been doing. If I am right, though, and Christians are hypocrites, we must recognize the gravity of our error and make the manifold necessary changes. If we do not, in many cases there will be, literally, hell to pay.

I was going to close with that, but I feel compelled to add a word of hope. Matthew 23 is the longest tirade Jesus shared against the Pharisees. At the end of it, though, Jesus shifts from the words of judgment to a message of tenderness:

> "Jerusalem, Jerusalem, who kills the prophets and stones those who are sent to her! How often I wanted to gather your children together, the way a hen gathers her chicks under her wings, and you were unwilling."[31]

Is this a word of sorrow or a word of hope? It depends on the response of those hearing the message. If those hearing Jesus' words retain their hearts of stone, then it is a word of sorrow that anticipates the judgment to come. If, however, those hearing it repent, it becomes a word of hope. Jesus is not just willing, He is eager to gather His children together and hold them close. The outcome for American Christians remains an open question.

Epilogue

"[They] Rejected God's Purpose for Themselves"

Repentance, John the Baptist, and what's next

If there was anyone during Jesus' life who should have had insight into His vision, it would have been John the Baptist. The forerunner of Christ as well as Jesus' cousin, John leapt in the womb when Jesus' mother arrived at his house.[1] As one reads the gospels, John seems to be the other guy on the scene who is in on this new thing that God is doing. That expectation is what makes John's question to Jesus in Luke 7 simply shocking:

> Summoning two of his disciples, John sent them to [Jesus], saying, "Are You the Expected One, or do we look for someone else?"[2]

Wow. We might expect one of the scribes to doubt that Jesus was the Messiah. We might even find it unsurprising if one of Jesus' disciples asked if He was the Christ, given their propensity for hardheadedness in spiritual matters. But John the Baptist? How could John have doubts about Jesus?

The most likely explanation begins with the general expectations about the Messiah. The Jews hated that they were ruled by the Romans. (Well, except for the Israelites who were profitably in collusion with Rome.) They looked with anticipation for God to send the promised Messiah, who would lead the Jews in throwing off their oppressive bonds. This is key: they expected a *political* revolution.

Because of this, when John was arrested by Herod and put in jail, I believe his thoughts were most likely something like: "All right, here we go!"[3] That is, he had been waiting on Jesus to cease this itinerate preaching thing and get to the business of taking over. When John was thrown in jail, he likely believed it was a sign the time had come. As thunder rumbling in the distance lets you know that the storm is approaching, John probably saw his arrest as a sign that events were ramping up to a decisive finale.

But then he was in jail a few days and nothing big happened. Then he was in jail for a few weeks and nothing big happened. He began wondering, "Why are things not breaking loose?" Over time, his doubts became sufficient that he called a couple of his disciples and sent them to Jesus with that question:

> "Are You the Expected One, or do we look for someone else?"[4]

You can feel the underlying push in his question. "If You are the guy, You are getting ready to start something, right?" "If You are the Messiah, what is the hold up?" The question is a cry from John: "Why are You not doing what I know You are going to do?"

Of course, the answer is that Jesus did not come with the intention of overthrowing Rome. Rather, the Bible teaches that He had a much grander ambition: to overthrow sin and death. He came as a Suffering Servant to accomplish that goal on the cross and in His resurrection. The problem was that *John's expectations of God's vision were fundamentally off.*

Jesus replied to John's ambassadors:

> "Go and report to John what you have seen and heard: the blind receive sight, the lame walk, the lepers are cleansed, and the deaf hear, the dead are raised up, the poor have the gospel preached to them. Blessed is he who does not take offense at Me."[5]

It is not that nothing was happening. There were miracles. There were prophecies being fulfilled. The poor and broken found teaching that brought them wholeness. But Jesus was not doing it in a way that fit John's preconceived expectations. John was so focused on the political expectations that he could not see God's movement for what it was.

This is a critical point: many times believers become so focused on their expectations of the way they think that God will move that they become blind to what God actually desires to do. It can happen when, like John, God is not bringing you the power and authority you were expecting. It can happen when the divine message does not fit with your comfortable, pre-existing theology. It can happen when the new message from God threatens your place in society. It can happen when you have been using the Bible to prove your point rather than to seek God's heart. It can happen when your hypocrisy blinds you to deeper spiritual truths.

This is, I believe, exactly where American Christians are now. They have become so focused on their expectations of the way that God will move that they are blind to what God actually desires to do. Christians are not merely one-off of having everything together spiritually – they are distant from God. Christians are not almost to their destination, but just running slightly behind – they are pointed in the wrong direction and have their pedal to the floor. The point of this book is not that Christians are close to having it right – it is that Christians are not even in the right ballpark. My goal for the reader of this book is not to believe that Christians need to make a few minor adjustments. My goal is that the reader believe that modern American conservative Christians are just like the Pharisees. Christians are just like the Pharisees.

Where To Now?

Some of you absolutely discount my analysis and conclusion. That is fine – you have that freedom. You can continue doing what you have been doing. What about those of you, though, who have a knot in your stomach right now with the thought, "He is right. Help us, Lord, he is right. We are just like the Pharisees." If that is true, what is next? Of course, it should go without saying that, concerning the truths shared in the preceding chapters, we should endeavor to be more like Christ and less like the Pharisees. I certainly encourage you to begin the difficult process of incorporating those truths into your spiritual walk. Beyond that, though, I do not have a comprehensive strategy or a four-point action plan. Actually, I think conservative Christians' propensity toward "pragmatic, actionable programs" is part of their problem. What I have to offer as I conclude is simply a starting point.

Back in Luke 7, after John the Baptist's two representatives left, Jesus turned to the crowd and complimented John:

> "I say to you, among those born of women there is no one greater than John; yet he who is least in the kingdom of God is greater than he."[6]

Pretty nice thing to have Jesus say about you. Immediately after that statement, there are two crucial verses:

> When all the people and the tax collectors heard this [about John], they acknowledged God's justice, having been baptized by John. But *the Pharisees* and the lawyers *rejected God's purpose for themselves*, not having been baptized by John.[7]

In John's preaching and invitation to be baptized, God gave the Pharisees an open door to get a little closer to clearly seeing and living out God's purposes for their lives, but they rejected that opportunity.

What was it about John's preaching to be baptized that they would not receive? John's preaching was centered on *repentance*:

> Now in those days John the Baptist came, preaching in the wilderness of Judea, saying, "*Repent*, for the kingdom of heaven is at hand."[8]

John's baptism was a baptism of *repentance*:

> "I baptize you with water for *repentance*."⁹

John's message to the Pharisees was a message of *repentance*:

> But when [John] saw many of the Pharisees . . . he said to them, "You brood of vipers, who warned you to flee from the wrath to come? Therefore bear fruit in keeping with *repentance*."¹⁰

Some of the Pharisees submitted their hearts to John's teaching, repented, and were baptized. Many, though, refused to repent, including those Jesus mentioned in Luke 7. The larger point in both cases is that the message John was preaching was a message of repentance.

Going back to the Luke 7 passage, when the Pharisees "rejected God's purpose for themselves," that action was a refusal to *repent*. They could not bring themselves to admit they were wrong. They could not bring themselves to concede they were distant from God and needed new direction. They could not bring themselves to submit to teaching that was not from their own mouths. Whatever the specific thought that held them back, the bottom line is that they refused to repent, despite the fact that it was God's will for their lives in that moment.

Some think of John the Baptist as the "repentance" preacher and that Jesus came along after him with a different message. In fact, the Bible says that Jesus continued John's message. When Jesus began His preaching after John had been arrested, we read:

> From that time Jesus began to preach and say, "*Repent*, for the kingdom of heaven is at hand."¹¹

When Jesus shared with the Pharisees what His mission was, He said:

> "I have not come to call the righteous but sinners to *repentance*."[12]

When Jesus sent out the twelve disciples to preach, the Bible tells us:

> [The disciples] went out and preached that people should *repent*.[13]

After His resurrection, Jesus gave His followers their mission statement:

> Then He opened their minds to understand the Scriptures, and He said to them, "Thus it is written, that the Christ would suffer and rise again from the dead the third day, and that *repentance* for forgiveness of sins would be proclaimed in His name to all the nations, beginning from Jerusalem."[14]

There are more references, but you get the idea.[15]

The fundamental message for both John the Baptist and Jesus was one of *repentance*. Repentance demands that you acknowledge that you do not know it all, that you have been wrong, that you are not doing what God wants, and that you need His mercy, forgiveness, and direction. It is a deeply humbling place to be. Many of the Pharisees would not go there and in their refusal they "rejected God's purpose for themselves."

Repentance is what Christians need. Repentance for our hypocrisy. Repentance for our love of power. Repentance for our failure to be Christlike. Repentance for our selective reading of the Bible. Repentance for our love of our traditions. Repentance for the many varied mistakes that this book has detailed. Christians need to acknowledge that we have been radically, breathtakingly, horribly off track and have in manifold ways dishonored God and His name with our lives. We need to acknowledge that we are responsible for diverting many people away from God. We need to acknowledge that we are not God's remnant; as it stands now, we are God's enemies.

Whether Christians will heed this painful message is an open question. It is a hopeful sign that there were some Pharisees who received Jesus' rebuke and repented. Certainly not enough, but there were some. I pray that far more Christians will heed this word and turn back to God. While I hold to the hope that many humbly will, it must be conceded that it would be a severe departure from their present path. They have invested much in the false way they are traveling.

If we are willing to repent, there will undoubtedly be the temptation to repent and then immediately jump back into action. That, in my opinion, would be a grave mistake. Repentant Christians need to wait on God. We need to dwell in our repentance for an extended period of time. This is a punishment, but it is also a spiritual necessity. We are so entrenched in our previous thinking and so distant from God's plan the gulf cannot quickly be covered. We need to pray, confessing our sins and admitting our mistakes. We need to deeply read the Word, attempting to see it with God's eyes instead of our standard theological interpretation. We need to quit believing that we have the right answers to all the questions and begin to see we not only are lacking the right answers, but also usually are not even asking the right questions. We need to lay aside our deeply held desire to be God's spokespeople on all religious issues and instead submit to the Holy Spirit's quiet guidance. There is still abundant reason to hope, but the path forward begins with contrition.

How long will this take? Years? A generation? I do not know. I do, however, know that the continuation of Christian life as it is presently constituted is not an acceptable option. In their refusal to repent, the Pharisees rejected God's purpose for their lives; if modern American conservative Christians refuse to repent, they too will be rejecting God's purpose for their lives. Now is the moment for them to decide if they will be Christian disciples or Christian Pharisees.

Author James Butcher welcomes comments or questions concerning *Christian Pharisees*. He can be contacted via www.ChristianPharisees.com.

Endnotes

Introduction
[1] Philip Yancey, *What's So Amazing About Grace*, Zondervan, 1997, p. 11.
[2] A church plant is starting a new congregation.
[3] Anthony Saldarini, *Pharisees, Scribes and Sadducees in Palestinian Society*, William B. Eerdmans Publishing Company, 1988, p. 144.
[4] "The State of the Church 2016," barna.org, September 15, 2016, accessed September 23, 2016. Interestingly, Barna further says, "Being classified as an evangelical is not dependent upon church attendance or the denominational affiliation of the church attended. Respondents were not asked to describe themselves as 'evangelical.'"

Chapter One: "Why Does Your Teacher Eat With Sinners?"
[1] Matthew 9:9 (NASB).
[2] Matthew 9:10 (NIV).
[3] Matthew 9:10 (NASB).
[4] Matthew 9:11 (NASB).
[55] R.J. Wyatt, "Pharisees," *The International Standard Bible Encyclopedia*, Volume Three, William B. Eerdmans Publishing Company, 1986, pp. 822-829.
[6] Luke 7:37-38 (NASB).
[7] Luke 7:38.
[8] Luke 7:39 (NASB).
[9] Matthew 9:12-13 (NASB).
[10] John 3:17 (NASB).
[11] Matthew 9:13 (NASB).
[12] Matthew 9:15 (NIV).
[13] Matthew 9:16-17 (NIV).
[14] Matthew 9:18.
[15] Matthew 9:20-21.
[16] Matthew 9:22.
[17] Matthew 9:23-25.
[18] Matthew 9:27 (NASB).
[19] Matthew 9:29 (NASB).
[20] Matthew 9:30.
[21] Matthew 9:32-33.
[22] Matthew 9:34 (NASB).
[23] Matthew 9:35 (NASB).
[24] Matthew 9:36 (NASB).
[25] Matthew 9:37-38 (NASB).
[26] Matthew 9:13 (NASB).
[27] Matthew 16:24-26, just to name one.

Chapter Two: "Whoever Exalts Himself Shall Be Humbled"
[1] Matthew 3:7 (NIV). The Sadducees were also coming out to see John the Baptist. The Bible does not specifically tell us how loudly John spoke these words to them, but given the nature of the message, I strongly believe that he said them loudly for everyone around to hear. John was no shrinking violet.
[2] Matthew 3:5-6; Luke 7:30.
[3] Matthew 3:4.
[4] Matthew 3:9-10 (NIV), emphasis added.
[5] Matthew 23:12 (NASB).
[6] Matthew 23:5 (NIV).
[7] Matthew 23:5 (NIV).
[8] Exodus 13:9 (NIV). See also Exodus 13:16, Deuteronomy 6:8; Deuteronomy 11:18.
[9] Numbers 15:38-39 (NIV).
[10] Matthew 5:15-16 (NIV).
[11] Matthew 6:1 (NIV).
[12] Matthew 23:6 (NASB).
[13] Matthew 23:7-9 (NIV).
[14] There is some concern that Paul later uses a couple of these terms in his letters in ways that initially seem to contradict Christ. In 1 Corinthians 4:15 he refers to himself as a spiritual "father." In 1 Timothy 2:7 and 2 Timothy 1:11 he uses the term "teacher." You could argue that in both cases he does not hold those as exalted titles but simply uses them as descriptive terms. The larger resolution of this issue, though, is beyond the interests of this book.
[15] Matthew 23:11 (NIV).
[16] Matthew 23:12 (NASB).
[17] Matthew 23:12 (NASB).
[18] Luke 14:7 (NIV). The prominent Pharisee is mentioned in verse 1.
[19] Luke 14:8-10 (NIV).
[20] Luke 14:11 (NIV).
[21] Matthew 7:12 (NASB).
[22] Luke 14:11 (NIV).
[23] Luke 14:12-14 (NIV).
[24] Luke 18:9 (NIV).
[25] Luke 18:10-12 (NIV).
[26] Luke 18:13 (NIV).
[27] Luke 18:14 (NIV).
[28] John 3:16 (NASB).
[29] Ephesians 2:8-9 (NIV), emphasis added.
[30] Romans 10:13.
[31] 2 Corinthians 5:17.
[32] John 14:15-17.
[33] John 10:10; John 3:16.

Chapter Three: "[They] Will Take Away Both Our Place and Our Nation"
[1] John 11:48 (NASB), emphasis added.

[2] Of course, the chapter divisions were not in the original text, although the way the chapters lie works well for the point I am making. Nonetheless, it still sits at the center of John even if the book is read without the chapter divisions.
[3] John 11:45 (NASB), emphasis added.
[4] John 11:47-48 (NASB), emphasis added.
[5] John 12:9-11 (NASB), emphasis added.
[6] The chief priests also included some Sadducees, who didn't believe in life after death, so they would have had a different motivation to be threatened by Lazarus.
[7] John 12:12; Luke 19:35. See Zechariah 9:9 also.
[8] John 12:14.
[9] John 12:17-18 (NASB).
[10] John 12:19 (NIV), emphasis added.
[11] Matthew 21:23-27; Mark 11:27-33; Luke 20:1-8.
[12] Mark 11:27-28 (NASB).
[13] Mark 11:29-30 (NASB).
[14] Mark 11:31-33 (NASB).
[15] Mark 11:32 (NASB).
[16] Mark 11:33.
[17] John 12:20-21 (NIV).
[18] John 12:24 (NIV), 32 (NASB).
[19] John 12:33 (NASB).
[20] John 12:36 (NIV).
[21] John 12:13 (NIV).
[22] See also John 6:15.
[23] John 12:42 (NASB).
[24] John 12:43 (NASB).
[25] John 13:3-5 (NASB).
[26] John 13:13-16 (NASB).
[27] Luke 22:25-27 (NASB).
[28] My reference to forty years arises from the transforming impact of the Roe v. Wade court decision in 1973 and the subsequent movement by conservative Christians into cultural and political engagement. Other historical frames of reference could be utilized. This is just the one that is useful for me in this discussion.
[29] Kevin Kruse, *One Nation Under God*, Basic Books, 2015, p. 68.
[30] Ibid.
[31] 1 Peter 2:9-10 (NIV), emphasis added.
[32] 2 Chronicles 7:14 (KJV).
[33] Kevin Kruse. *One Nation Under God*, Basic Books, 2015, p. xv, emphasis added.
[34] Ibid, pp. 67-93.
[35] When Eisenhower was inaugurated in 1953, one of the two Bibles he used was open to 2 Chronicles 7:14. Jon Meacham, *American Gospel*, Random House, 2006, p. 271.
[36] Kevin Kruse. *One Nation Under God*, Basic Books, 2015, p. 68.
[37] Ibid.
[38] Ibid, p. 73.

[39] "People & Ideas: Jerry Falwell," pbs.org, accessed 4/20/2016. http://www.pbs.org/godinamerica/people/jerry-falwell.html
[40] Matthew 7:13-14 (NIV), emphasis added.
[41] Matthew 5:13-14 (NIV).
[42] John 19:10 (NIV).
[43] John 18:36 (NASB).
[44] Matthew 26:52-53 (NASB).
[45] John 3:16-17 (NASB), emphasis added.
[46] Matthew 28:19-20 (NIV).
[47] Matthew 28:18 (KJV), emphasis added.
[48] John 12:36 (NIV).

Chapter Four: "A People Who Will Produce Its Fruit"
[1] Matthew 21:43 (NIV), emphasis added.
[2] John 15:5 (NASB), emphasis added.
[3] John 15:8 (NASB), emphasis added.
[4] Galatians 5:22-23 (NASB), emphasis added.
[5] Matthew 21:33-46.
[6] Matthew 21:43 (NIV), emphasis added.
[7] Matthew 21:45.
[8] Matthew 21:45 (NASB), emphasis added.
[9] Luke 13:6-9 (NIV), emphasis added.
[10] Luke 3:9 (NIV).
[11] Mark 11:12-14 (NASB), emphasis added. I have left out the comment that "it was not the season for figs" (verse 13) because it is distracting and is not necessary to the point I am trying to make.
[12] Just to cite the most prominent issue, there is a major difference between the version of the story in Matthew and Mark concerning when the fig tree withers. I intend to handle this in my next book, which will be on inerrancy.
[13] Mark 11:20-21 (NASB), emphasis added.
[14] Just so everyone is on the same page: the "cursing" here was not foul language, but speaking judgment.
[15] Just to cite a few additional examples of sandwiches in Mark: 1. Family versus enemy (Bread: Mark 3:20-21; Meat: Mark 3:22-30; Bread: Mark 3:31-35); 2. Insider versus outcast (Bread: Mark 5:21-24; Meat: Mark 5:25-34; Bread: Mark 5:35-43); 3. Transition to the new Kingdom (Bread: Mark 6:6b-13; Meat: Mark 6:14-29; Bread: Mark 6:30-31); 4. The plot and the plan (Bread: Mark 14:1-2; Meat: Mark 14:3-9; Bread: Mark 14:10-11).
[16] Mark 11:15-18 (NASB), emphasis added.
[17] "Many Churchgoers and Faith Leaders Struggle to Define Spiritual Maturity," study released 5/11/2009, barna.org, site accessed 3/9/2016.
[18] David Kinnaman, *UnChristian*, Baker, 2007, pp. 182-3.
[19] Ibid, pp. 48.
[20] Matthew 7:13-14 (NIV).
[21] "New Research on the State of Discipleship," study released 12/1/2015, barna.org, site accessed 3/9/2016.

[22] "Many Churchgoers and Faith Leaders Struggle to Define Spiritual Maturity," study released 5/11/2009, barna.org, site accessed 3/9/2016.
[23] A.T. Robertson, *The Pharisees and Jesus: the Stone Lectures for 1915-16*, p. 38.
[24] Ibid.
[25] Matthew 23:4 (NIV).
[26] A.T. Robertson, *The Pharisees and Jesus: the Stone Lectures for 1915-16*, pp. 45-46.
[27] Matthew 12:9-10 (NASB), emphasis added.
[28] Matthew 12:11-12 (NASB), emphasis added.
[29] Matthew 12:14 (NASB).
[30] Romans 10:9 (NASB), emphasis added.
[31] Matthew 7:21 (NASB), emphasis added.
[32] See, for examples, John 10:27 and John 12:26.
[33] Luke 13:6-9 (NIV), emphasis added.
[34] Matthew 7:15-20 (NIV), emphasis added.
[35] Luke 3:9 (NIV). Obviously, in these passages "cut down" and "thrown into the fire" are intended as images to be understood as hell.
[36] 1 Corinthians 3:11-15 (NASB), emphasis added.
[37] An example of what this might look like. A pastor is at a church for a decade and sees the congregation grow. That gives the initial appearance of being fruitful. However, when he stands before God at judgment, it is revealed that his entire motivation was his own pride and fame. Because of that, when he was praised in his earthly life, he received his "reward in full" (see Matthew 6:2, 5, 16 (NIV)). He did the right thing but with the wrong motive.
[38] Matthew 21:43 (NIV), emphasis added.
[39] Matthew 21:45 (NASB), emphasis added.
[40] Matthew 25:40 (NIV).
[41] Matthew 25:31-32 (NASB).
[42] Matthew 25:34-36 (NASB).
[43] Matthew 25:40 (NIV).
[44] Matthew 25:45-46 (NIV).
[45] Matthew 7:15-18 (NIV), emphasis added.
[46] 2 Corinthians 3:18, to cite one example.
[47] Matthew 7:21 (NASB), emphasis added.
[48] Matthew 7:24-25 (NIV), emphasis added.
[49] Synoptic refers to the gospels of Matthew, Mark, and Luke.
[50] Matthew 13:3-8 (NIV).
[51] Matthew 13:19 (NIV).
[52] Matthew 13:20-21 (NIV).
[53] Matthew 13:22 (NIV).
[54] This is troubling to some Baptists, who believe in eternal security, because one of the phrases the passage uses is "falls away" and that sounds dangerously close to the idea of "losing your salvation." Eternal security (the idea that a Christian cannot "lose" their salvation) is fundamental to Baptists. There are two reasons, though, that this passage is clearly intended to be understood as having the first three seeds represent non-believers and the final seed represent true followers of Christ. First, as this chapter indicates through an abundance of Scripture

references, fruitfulness is a defining characteristic of a true follower of Christ. The first three seeds lacked fruitfulness and therefore cannot be Christians. Secondly, in the Sermon on the Mount, Jesus stated that His path required going through a "small" gate and walking a "narrow" road. This means that the number of Christians will be small.

[55] Matthew 13:8 (NIV).
[56] John 15:5, 8 (NIV), emphasis added.
[57] Luke 8:15 (NIV). The "good soil" might be difficult for some to understand. How can someone be "good soil" if all humanity is tainted by sin? I would argue that the Bible's intent here is that anyone can become "good soil" by genuinely and openly inviting Jesus into their life, upon which He changes them into a new creation (see Romans).
[58] John MacArthur, *Matthew 8-15*, Moody Press, 1987, pp. 346-347.
[59] John 15:1 (NIV).
[60] John 15:1, 5 (NIV).
[61] John 15:2 (NASB), emphasis added.
[62] John 15:4 (NASB), emphasis added.
[63] John 15:5 (NASB), emphasis added.
[64] John 15:8 (NASB), emphasis added.
[65] John 15:4-5 (NASB), emphasis added.
[66] John 15:10 (NASB), emphasis added.
[67] John 15:5 (NASB).
[68] One approach that I have found helpful concerns the three places in the gospel of John where Jesus essentially says, "If you do this, then you're really My disciple." Those three places are John 8:31-32, John 13:35, and John 15:8. John 8:31-32 (NASB) reads, "So Jesus was saying to those Jews who had believed Him, 'If you continue in My word, then you are truly disciples of Mine; and you will know the truth, and the truth will make you free.'" This points toward knowing Jesus' teaching ("word"), so I would argue that deeply knowing the Bible would be where to start in pursuing that. John 13:35 (NASB) reads, "By this all men will know that you are My disciples, if you have love for one another." This points toward investing in people with our time, love, and money. That is, love as more than "think nice thought toward" but rather actually showing love in practical ways. John 15:8 (NASB) reads, "My Father is glorified in this, that you bear much fruit, and so prove to be My disciples." This points us toward actively serving.

Chapter Five: "He Who Is Forgiven Little Loves Little"
[1] Luke 7:36-37, 40.
[2] Luke 7:37-38 (NIV).
[3] Luke 7:39 (NASB).
[4] Luke 7:41-42 (NIV).
[5] Luke 7:42 (NIV).
[6] Luke 7:43 (NIV).
[7] Luke 7:44-47 (NASB).
[8] Matthew 22:36-40.
[9] Ephesians 2:8-9.

[10] Matthew 9:11.
[11] Romans 6:1-2 (NASB).
[12] Matthew 21:31 (NASB).
[13] Matthew 21:32 (NIV).
[14] Matthew 11:19 (NASB).
[15] 1 Timothy 1:15 (NASB).
[16] 1 Timothy 1:16 (NASB).
[17] Luke 7:47 (NASB).
[18] James 4:6; 1 Peter 5:5.

Chapter Six: "You Are Israel's Teacher and Do You Not Understand These Things?"
[1] John 3:1 (NIV).
[2] John 3:2 (NIV).
[3] John 3:2 (NASB).
[4] John 3:3 (NIV).
[5] John 3:4 (NIV).
[6] John 3:5-8 (NIV).
[7] John 3:9 (NIV).
[8] John 3:10 (NIV).
[9] John 3:11-15 (NIV).
[10] Some argue that the plural is a reference to the Trinity. That is certainly possible, though I think the argument I share is stronger.
[11] John 3:10 (NIV).
[12] Romans 2:1 (NASB).
[13] Romans 3:10 (NIV).
[14] Romans 5:8 (NASB).
[15] Romans 6:6 (NASB).
[16] 2 Corinthians 5:17 (NIV), emphasis added.
[17] Ezekiel 36:26 (NIV), emphasis added.
[18] Romans 8:5-9; Romans 13:14; Galatians 5:19-21, 24; Galatians 6:8; Ephesians 2:3.
[19] John 16:7 (NASB).
[20] Romans 8:14 (NASB).
[21] "How to Know God Personally," cru.org, accessed 3/4/3016.
[22] Jeremiah 29:11 (NIV).
[23] See Matthew 5:11-12; Matthew 16:24-25; Galatians 6:2.
[24] Interestingly, of all the points in the entire presentation, that is the only one without a Scripture cited to support it.
[25] "Begin Your Journey To Peace," peacewithgod.net, accessed 3/4/2016. This is the site that visitors to billygraham.org are sent to when they click on the "How to Know Jesus" tab.
[26] An additional factor to consider regarding evangelicals' lack of fruitfulness is the comfort level of American evangelicals living the American Dream. Although this idea is more fully unpacked in the chapter on the Pharisees as "lovers of money," it is worth brief consideration here as well. Part of the reason that American evangelicals do not have a vision for a spiritual fruitfulness is that they are often

content in the material prosperity that goes with the American Dream. Seeing spiritual fruitfulness could be called a sign of spiritual "success," in the sense that you are seeing God move in and through you. Many American evangelicals are distracted by material "success," defined as achieving "the good life." Because of that, they are content, or too distracted by, with their materially "successful" lives and may not see their stark failing to produce what Jesus said He desired – spiritual fruitfulness.

As noted in that chapter, the values of the American Dream and the Kingdom of God are antithetical. You cannot pursue the values of one without it intrinsically taking you further from the values of the other. Many American Christians believe they have lived a "fruitful" life because they have achieved a decent measure of the American Dream, failing to realize that has little to do with the fruitfulness that Jesus desires from our lives.

[27] Matthew 7:21 (NASB), emphasis added.
[28] Matthew 7:24 (NIV), emphasis added.
[29] Matthew 12:50 (NASB), emphasis added.
[30] John 7:17 (NIV), emphasis added.
[31] John 14:21 (NASB), emphasis added.
[32] John 14:23 (NASB), emphasis added.
[33] John 15:10 (NASB), emphasis added.
[34] Matthew 16:25 (NASB). See also Mark 8:35 and Luke 9:24.
[35] Matthew 16:24 (NASB). See also Mark 8:34 and Luke 9:23.
[36] Matthew 16:24 (NASB). See also Mark 8:34 and Luke 9:23.
[37] Matthew 23:12; Luke 14:11.
[38] Matthew 5:1-12.
[39] Matthew 16:26; Mark 8:36; Luke 9:25.
[40] Matthew 6:16-34.

Chapter Seven: "You Do Not Know the Scriptures"

[1] I had never heard about that practice before and thought he was saying "youth in Asia."
[2] John 7:32.
[3] John 7:45-46 (NASB).
[4] John 7:47-49 (NASB).
[5] John 7:50. The meeting is John 3:1-21.
[6] John 7:7-8, 10 (NIV).
[7] John 7:51 (NIV).
[8] John 7:52 (NIV).
[9] Jonah (2 Kings 14:25; Jonah 1:1); Elijah (1 Kings 17:1); Micah (Micah 1:1).
[10] "By Scripture alone." The Protestant Reformation argued that tradition was not of equal authority with Scripture, but that the church should look to Scripture alone as its foundation and truth.
[11] Matthew 22:15-16 (NASB).
[12] Matthew 22:18-22 (NIV), emphasis added.
[13] Stephen R. Covey, *The 7 Habits of Highly Effective People*, Simon & Schuster, p. 239.
[14] Ephesians 6:17 is the verse most are referring to in using this phrase.

[15] Within this, there is a second, peripheral issue that is worth considering: the duplicity the Pharisees use. Not only do they come with a poor motive, but they then lie as part of their presentation:

> "Teacher, we know that You are truthful
> and teach the way of God in truth, and defer to no one;
> for You are not partial to any. Tell us then, what do you think?"[15]

These are the words the Pharisees open with before asking their question about paying taxes to Caesar. They are, of course, lying. They do not believe Jesus is "truthful," teaches "the way of God in truth," defers "to no one," and is not "partial to any." They hate Him and are doing everything they can to destroy Him. The nicest phrase you could use here is false flattery, but it deserves a simpler moniker: lying. Again, they are coming to Jesus convinced they are doing God's will in opposing Him. They lie presumably because they believe this friendly introduction will make it more likely Jesus will freely respond with one of the two desired answers. They come believing they are doing God's will and they believe it is justified to lie in order to reach the result they desire. *They are trying to accomplish a godly end by non-godly means.*

Do conservative Christians do the same thing? Have you ever been involved in a church fight in an evangelical church? Both sides see what they stand for as "God's will" for their church. The situation descends quickly into gossip, malice, lies, deception, and treachery. Each side is attempting to accomplish what they see as a Christian end by non-Christian means. Each side justifies, say, the gossip they are spreading with the fact that the other side is doing the same thing and *we have to win this fight for the sake of our church.* The truth, though, is that it is never acceptable to use non-Christian means to attempt to accomplish Christian ends.

Similar things happen on a larger scale when there are issues that threaten to split a denomination. The lack of kindness and generosity toward "the other side" is generally almost immediate and gets increasingly pronounced as the situation continues.

Similar things sometimes happen on a personal scale when two conservative Christians disagree theologically. They will continue to claw at each other and demean the other's views long after the initial argument.

In each context, conservative Christians try to accomplish a "godly end" (defined as winning this argument or battle for Jesus by proving their own theological beliefs to be right) by "non-godly means" (gossip, deception, etc. – whatever it takes to win).

[16] Matthew 22:24-28 (NIV).
[17] Presumably, given the frequency of polygamy in the Old Testament, it would not be the same theological problem in the minds of the Sadducees if it were one man married to seven sisters. (On the other hand, although one man married to seven sisters might not create a theological problem for the Sadducees, I would expect it to create substantial domestic problems for the man.)
[18] Matthew 22:29 (NIV).

[19] Matthew 22:30-32 (NIV).
[20] This is, to my mind, not a particularly strong argument, given that the presence of Abraham alive in a spiritual heaven is not the same thing as saying that Abraham would be resurrected to a physical body someday. The verb tense does not require one to go that further step. It would, however, stand against the idea that once people died they completely cease to exist. Further, there are Old Testament passages that point in both directions (that there is continued existence and that the end of life in this world is the end of existence).
[21] Matthew 22:41-42 (NASB).
[22] Matthew 22:42.
[23] See, for example, Luke 2:4.
[24] Matthew 22:43-45 (NASB).
[25] Matthew 22:46 (NASB).
[26] Matthew 22:34-36 (NIV).
[27] Matthew 22:37-40 (NIV).
[28] John 1:1 (NASB).
[29] John 17:20-23.
[30] John 17:20-21 (NIV), emphasis added.
[31] John 17:23 (NIV).

Chapter Eight: "The Tradition of the Elders"
[1] Mark 7:3-4 (NASB), emphasis added.
[2] Mark 7:5 (NASB), emphasis added.
[3] Mark 7:8 (NASB), emphasis added.
[4] Mark 7:9 (NASB), emphasis added.
[5] Mark 7:10 (NASB).
[6] Mark 7:9-13 (NASB).
[7] 1 Corinthians 12:14 (NASB).
[8] 1 Corinthians 12:18-20 (NASB).
[9] 1 Timothy 2:9-10 (NIV).
[10] Matthew 23:28 (NIV).
[11] Galatians 2:1-10.
[12] Galatians 2:10 (NASB).
[13] Matthew 25:34-36 (NASB).
[14] Matthew 25:40 (NASB).
[15] Matthew 23:14 (NASB). The phrase also appears in Mark 12:40 and Luke 20:47.
[16] Acts 6:1-7.
[17] Acts 6:1.
[18] The church plant I pastored attempted to address these questions, with a vision of having no physical building and of giving at least fifty percent of our income to ministries outside the church.
[19] Certainly this is a challenging problem for churches that have long been structured in this traditional way. Still, progress can be made. What can be done to decrease building expenses? Can the church made a deliberate effort to expand the percentage of the church budget that is spent on these compassion expenses? Often, desires to construct additional buildings need to be reconsidered. And, of

course, denominations need to prioritize church plants that are structured more effectively.
[20] 1 Corinthians 1:27 (NASB).
[21] John 1:46 (NASB).
[22] 1 Samuel 16:9-13.
[23] Luke 14:11 (NASB).
[24] Matthew 7:13-14 (NIV).
[25] John 6:66-67 (NIV).
[26] Ephesians 4:13 (NLT).
[27] Ephesians 1:17-19 (NIV).
[28] 2 Thessalonians 1:11-12 (NIV).
[29] John 17:15, 17 (NASB).
[30] Acts 6:1-3.
[31] Acts 6:4 (NASB).
[32] Matthew 21:13 (NASB), emphasis added.
[33] 1 Corinthians 14:26 (NIV).
[34] See, for instance, Acts 20:17, 28 and Titus 1:5.
[35] Exodus 20:8-11 (NIV).
[36] Matthew 9:9 (NASB), emphasis added.
[37] Matthew 7:21 (NASB), emphasis added.
[38] Mark 7:9, 13 (NIV).

Chapter Nine: "Lovers of Money"
[1] Luke 18:18-23.
[2] Luke 18:24-25 (NASB).
[3] Luke 18:26 (NASB).
[4] Luke 16:14 (NASB).
[5] Luke 16:24 (NASB), emphasis added.
[6] Luke 16:15 (NASB).
[7] Luke 16:1-2 (NASB).
[8] Luke 15:3 (NASB).
[9] Luke 16:4-7 (NASB).
[10] Luke 16:8 (NASB), emphasis added.
[11] Luke 16:8-9 (NASB), emphasis added.
[12] Luke 16:10-11 (NASB).
[13] Frank Honeycutt, *Preaching to Skeptics and Seekers*, Abingdon Press, 2001.
[14] Luke 16:12 (NASB).
[15] 1 Corinthians 6:20; 1 Corinthians 7:23.
[16] Matthew 25:21 (NKJV).
[17] Matthew 25:14-15 (NLT).
[18] Matthew 25:19-20 (NLT).
[19] Luke 19:16-17 (NLT).
[20] Matthew 13:23 (NIV).
[21] Matthew 21:33 (NLT).
[22] Matthew 21:34 (NLT).
[23] Matthew 21:43 (NIV).

24 "American Donor Trends," 6/3/2013, barna.org, accessed 10/26/2016. "Among born again Christians, which includes both evangelicals and non-evangelicals, 12% tithed in 2012, which his on par with the average for the past decade." No statistics were available for only evangelicals. Barna defines evangelicals narrowly, so if you include those claiming to be evangelicals despite the lack of evidence, the percentage of tithers would be lower.
25 "The Truth About Christians Tithing In The U.S.", 12/21/2015, sharefaith.com, accessed 10/26/2016.
26 "What Would Happen if the Church Tithed?", Mike Holmes, 3/8/2016, relevantmagazine.com, accessed 10/26/2016.
27 Luke 16:15 (NASB).
28 Luke 16:14 (NASB), emphasis added.
29 Hebrews 13:5 (NIV).
30 Hebrews 13:5 (NIV).
31 1 Timothy 6:6-7 (NIV).
32 1 Timothy 6:9 (NIV).
33 1 Timothy 6:10 (NIV).
34 Luke 6:24-25 (NIV).
35 Luke 12:16-22.
36 Luke 12:20 (NIV).
37 Luke 12:21 (NIV).
38 Luke 12:15 (NIV).

Chapter Ten: "Woe to You, You Hypocrites"
1 Luke 12:1 (NIV), emphasis added.
2 Matthew 16:6, 11-12; Mark 8:15; Luke 12:1.
3 Matthew 16:12 (NIV).
4 Matthew 6:2 (NIV), emphasis added.
5 Matthew 6:5 (NIV), emphasis added.
6 Matthew 7:3-5 (NIV), emphasis added.
7 Matthew 23:13, 15, 16, 23, 25, 27, 29 (NIV).
8 Luke 11:45 (NIV).
9 Luke 11:46 (NIV).
10 Matthew 23:13 (NIV), emphasis added.
11 Matthew 23:4 (NIV).
12 Best known from the seminal DC Talk album "Jesus Freak."
13 Matthew 23:13 (NIV).
14 Matthew 23:15 (NIV), emphasis added. Verse 14 is not in the best manuscripts and so most modern translations exclude it.
15 Matthew 28:18-19 (NASB).
16 Matthew 23:16-22 (NIV).
17 Matthew 5:37 (NIV).
18 Matthew 8:20 (NIV).
19 Matthew 23:23-24 (NIV).
20 Leviticus 11:4, 42.

[21] Emily L. Hauser, "The gobsmacking racism of America's criminal justice system," theweek.com, May 27, 2016.
[22] Chelsea Patterson, "Getting involved in foster care by serving families," erlc.com, June 6, 2016.
[23] Bob Smietana, "Statistical Illusion," christianitytoday.com, April 1, 2006.
[24] James 1:27 (NIV), emphasis added.
[25] "4012. pistis," *The Complete Word Study Dictionary*, ed. Spiros Zodhiates, AIG International, Inc., 1992, pp. 1162-1164.
[26] This is a familiar term in evangelical circles. It's comparable to a pet being "house-broken."
[27] Matthew 23:25-26 (NIV), emphasis added.
[28] Mark 7:4 (NIV).
[29] Matthew 23:27-28 (NIV), emphasis added.
[30] Matthew 23:29-31 (NIV), emphasis added.
[31] Matthew 23:37 (NASB).

Epilogue: "[They] Rejected God's Purposes for Themselves"
[1] Matthew 3:3; Luke 7:27; Luke 1:36; Luke 1:41-44.
[2] Luke 7:19 (NASB).
[3] Matthew 14:3.
[4] Luke 7:19 (NASB).
[5] Luke 7:22 (NASB).
[6] Luke 7:28 (NASB).
[7] Luke 7:29-30 (NASB).
[8] Matthew 3:1-2 (NASB), emphasis added.
[9] Matthew 3:11 (NASB), emphasis added.
[10] Matthew 3:7-8 (NASB), emphasis added.
[11] Matthew 4:17 (NASB), emphasis added. See also Mark 1:14-15.
[12] Luke 5:32 (NASB), emphasis added.
[13] Matthew 6:12 (NIV), emphasis added.
[14] Luke 24:45-47 (NASB), emphasis added.
[15] Matthew 11:20-21; Matthew 12:41; Luke 13:3, 5; Luke 10:13; Luke 11:32; Luke 15:7, 10; Luke 16:30.

www.ingramcontent.com/pod-product-compliance
Lightning Source LLC
Chambersburg PA
CBHW071906290426
44110CB00013B/1292